Brian McNeil CRV

THE MASTER IS HERE

Biblical Reflections
on Eucharistic Adoration

VERITAS

First published 1997 by
Veritas Publications
7-8 Lower Abbey Street
Dublin 1

ISBN 1 85390 312 4

British Library Cataloguing
in Publication Data.
A catalogue record for
this book is available
from the British Library.

Cover design by Bill Bolger
Printed in the Republic of Ireland by Betaprint Ltd, Dublin

CONTENTS

To my confrère
Gunther Jäger

Jesus Christ is the same
yesterday and today and forever
(Hb 13:8)

INTRODUCTION

All over the world today, we are experiencing a quiet but very vigorous flowering of eucharistic adoration. Parishes rediscover it, young people discover it for the first time. Many of the religious communities and prayer groups which came into existence in the years after the Second Vatican Council practise prolonged hours of silent adoration in front of the monstrance. Exposition has been detached from benediction (which is reserved to priests and deacons), and this means that the Blessed Sacrament can be exposed by women and men religious or even, in some of the new spiritual movements in the Church, by individual laypersons or groups in small house-chapels. An enormous declericalisation has taken place here in recent years, although its herald in the twentieth century was himself a priest: Charles de Foucauld in his Saharan hermitage (d.1916). We have come a long way since the Plenary Council held at Fort Augustus in 1886, which strictly forbade the Scottish parish priests to give eucharistic benediction without the explicit permission of the local bishop.

This development is surprising – to put it mildly! – to those who recall the period immediately after the Council, when various factors contributed in many parishes and religious communities to a diminution or even the disappearance of eucharistic adoration. In part, this was because eucharistic adoration and benediction of the Blessed Sacrament had often functioned as a substitute for the celebration of the Mass, as an opportunity to have an evening act of worship. Less than thirty years ago, evening Masses were still relatively uncommon and the churches were well-attended for benediction, which was usually preceded by the Rosary or (especially in Lent) the Stations of the Cross. Increased possibilities of celebrating evening Masses came at the same time as the positive experience of the centrality of the celebration as a dynamic *act* of worship, in a language everyone could understand.

This meant an immensely significant shift in spirituality from paraliturgy like exposition and benediction to the Mass itself, which was increasingly expected to satisfy all our religious needs. The renewed liturgical celebrations also involved a shift in emphasis in church architecture, so that the tabernacle very often was removed physically from the centre of the sanctuary – in some churches you have to look rather hard, if you want to know where to genuflect, and in others (like the cathedral in Munich) there is no sanctuary lamp to be seen anywhere, since the tabernacle is in a separate chapel behind a closed door. Add to this the importance attached to the ecumenical dimension of worship (which made eucharistic adoration appear a divisive form of prayer), and we have a climate in which many could plausibly assert that the traditional forms of eucharistic piety were dying or dead. Negative factors, such as a dismissal or at least a radical questioning of the value of contemplation in today's world – very typical in the second half of the 1960s – also played an important role here.

There was indeed something of a rekindling of the practice of eucharistic adoration from about the mid-1970s, but this did not lead to any genuinely widespread reflowering, because it was confined to particular groups within the Church who deliberately promoted adoration in a *partisan* manner, as a badge of doctrinal conservatism. I remember going into the church of St Etienne-du-Mont in Paris in October 1981, and finding it full of people taking part in eucharistic adoration. Three women dressed like the Lourdes Madonna in veils and long white gowns with blue sashes stood at the entrance of the church to hand out leaflets. I took one, and learned that their group held that the remedy for all the progressive ills of the Church lay in an emphatic devotion to what they called the 'three whitenesses', i.e. the Host, Mary and the Pope – an allusion to the Japanese Christians who reassured themselves of the orthodoxy of the first European missionaries to penetrate their country in the 1860s by asking them if they believed in precisely these three realities. This hijacking of eucharistic devotion was also a factor that turned many in the Church away from discovering for themselves the positive spiritual help it could give.

All in all, then, one could have felt pretty safe in prophesying, fifteen years ago or so, that eucharistic adoration would go the way of other forms of devotion in Church history, and simply disappear. And yet, things turned out very differently. The causes are difficult to identify and quantify, as they lie below the surface of Church life, where the Holy Spirit stirs our depths; we stand too close in time to the profound changes in the years after the Council to be able to analyse them fully. We can, however, see at least some of their fruits. This book is one symptom of the change that has taken place. It is born of the experience of eucharistic adoration in a small monastery in Norway, and its aim is to encourage others in the Church to open themselves to the same kind of experience. For the Christian life is something to be lived, and the living Christ calls us to find the fullness of life in the experience of his love.

* * *

The emphasis on *experience* is deliberate, and will in fact be the central theme of this book. It would have been possible to write a completely different book, one that concentrated on the doctrine and the theological justification of eucharistic adoration. But it suffices to quote only one dogmatic text here, which expresses succinctly the theological presupposition of everything that follows in this book. *Adoration of the Blessed Sacrament is in the most direct sense of the word a personal encounter with the living Jesus Christ,* because, in the words of the Council of Trent (1551): 'All who believe in Christ, according to the custom which has always been in force in the Catholic Church, should show this most holy sacrament in their veneration the worship of adoration (*latriae cultum*) which is owed to the true God. [...] For we believe that in it is present the same God whom the eternal Father brought into the world with the words: "And let all the angels of God adore him" (Hb 1:6), before whom the Magi fell down in adoration (Mt 2:11), and who, according to the testimony of scripture, was adored by the apostles in Galilee (Mt 28:17).'

Historically speaking, it seems to me perfectly arguable that this fundamental theological argument depends on the experience of the presence of Christ in the sacrament. The earliest accounts we have of the Christian liturgy in the second and third centuries tell us that the sacrament was taken by deacons to the sick who were unable to be present at Mass (see Justin, first *Apology,* chapter 65) and that lay people took the sacrament home so that they could receive communion on weekdays, when no Mass was celebrated (see Tertullian, *To his wife,* chapter 2). This means that the Church has grasped from the very beginning that Christ makes so absolute a gift of himself in the eucharist that his sacramental presence is not limited to the time of the celebration of the liturgy, but endures. It seems to me an entirely natural instinct, if one believes in this abiding presence of Christ's gift of himself, to turn to him in the sacramental elements and pray to him. Particular forms of prayer such as eucharistic adoration of the Host in a monstrance, and theological reflection on this, took time to develop, but ultimately they are generated, and continuously nourished, by the experience of the living Lord in the sacrament of the altar – an experience which has always existed in the Church, and which remains available today.

Reflections on texts from the Bible play a large part in this book. The amount of scriptural detail may seem unusual and unexpected in a book about eucharistic adoration, but it is absolutely essential for a solid foundation for speaking about this form of prayer. The best way to read this book is to take time to see each scene from the Gospels, perhaps to pause at the end of each quotation, and let the biblical words echo and set up their own network of resonances in us. (The same is true of the poets who are quoted in this book.) Let me say briefly how I approach the scriptural texts which are quoted here.

The Letter to the Hebrews says not only that Jesus is alive or that he acts today, but that he 'is the same yesterday and today and forever' (13:8). This means that he is not going to act or speak today in a way that would contradict what the Gospels tell us about him. On the contrary, the stories of scripture provide us with reliable images of how he will act today and in the future. This is true whether or not critical scholarship justifiably calls into question the historicity of particular details in these narratives, because what is involved is the communication to us of significant patterns that help us to discern how the unchanging God relates to us.

Thus, the important point is not whether what these narratives relate really happened. Sometimes we have very good reasons for concluding that an entire biblical narrative is what we call fiction, as with the Books of Tobit and Judith. This does not prevent them from being a valid revelation of how God acts today in our own lives, any more than the parables of Jesus would be somehow disqualified because the stories he tells did not really happen, or his words in the Gospel of John would be disqualified because (in the judgement of all serious scholars) they are not a literal record of things he really said.

This means that the words of scripture, originally spoken or written down in the quite specific historical situations to which they were directly addressed, take on a universal significance. Without detaching them from their original history, the Holy Spirit breathes life into them so that they can be the living word that speaks to us today in an unending variety of concrete situations.

In the case of eucharistic adoration, the text from Trent quoted above is an example of the application of a significant scriptural pattern to our own lives: the adoration of Jesus by the angels, the Magi and the apostles indicates the attitude required of us today in our encounter with him in the sacrament of the altar, since it is *the same Jesus* who is present.

*   *   *

The structure of this book is threefold. In the first part, I speak of the experience of eucharistic adoration and of what 'exposition' ought to mean: namely, our exposure to the healing love of Christ. In the second, I look at serious objections of a spiritual nature that have been raised to the practice of eucharistic adoration. In the third and final part, I say something about the deepest fruit of this prayer: namely, a configuration to Jesus that takes the form of a true compassion which offers hope to the suffering world.

This book is dedicated with gratitude to the brother with whom I prayed in my years in Norway. A first draft was written in Hammerfest, the northernmost town in the world, at the time of year when the sun never rises in the far north of Norway. I am grateful to my friends Nina Samuelsen and Father Wojciech Egiert MSF for making my stay possible, and to the Little Sisters of Jesus and all the others who keep the light of faith burning in the arctic darkness.

St Peter's, Munich
14 September 1996
Feast of the Exaltation of the Cross

PART ONE

THE EXPERIENCE

1

DISCOVERING ADORATION

Until some years ago, I had experienced adoration as a very formal act of worship in churches where the host was exposed in an ornate monstrance raised up so far away from the congregation that what one saw was a picture of remote splendour – gold and candles and flowers, the priest's brocaded cope, and spiralling clouds of incense. It was seldom possible actually to see the host, unless one happened to be one of the altar-servers. There was no moment of silence during the service of benediction: the whole time was filled with music or spoken prayers.

In our monastery, exposition and benediction were tacked on to evening prayer on Sundays and feast days, and lasted on average about seven minutes. When a longer exposition took place in the parish church, and I volunteered (or was told by my novice-master) to be present for a set period, it was assumed that I would take a prayer book, or perhaps a work of spirituality by Henri Nouwen or Cardinal Carlo Martini, to read during the periods of silence. The only time my eyes left the printed page was when I looked at my watch to see how much longer I would have to stay in the church. No one ever suggested to me that adoration could take the form of a simple prolonged act of looking at the host.

When I became a priest in 1985 and ministered in Italy and Germany, I found myself conducting the service of benediction relatively often. I frequently had the feeling, if I tried to insert a brief period of silent prayer as I knelt in front of the altar, that those behind me were making a silent telepathic protest: 'Get on with it!' So my experience of eucharistic worship was basically of an item on the spiritual programme that had to be done, not of a form of prayer that truly attracted me.

I began daily silent eucharistic adoration because people whom I respected recommended it to me. And perhaps it is good to

mention here, right at the beginning of this book, that it is not
my intention in any way to deny the value of the more traditional
forms: on the contrary, it was precisely the experience of silent
eucharistic adoration that led me to appreciate the value of the
Corpus Christi processions we have through the streets of
Munich and of the processions in our church here on Thursdays
(commemorating the institution of the sacrament on Holy
Thursday), of exposition and benediction in a large church, and
of the worship of those religious communities which sing the
Divine Office before the exposed Host; and likewise the value of
what we might call the non-visual form of adoration, namely
silent prayer before the tabernacle. All genuine forms of Christian
prayer and spirituality are complementary. Since they all lead to the
one Christ, they can never be in competition with one another.

* * *

If my experience in the last years has been very different from
earlier on, this came about initially for practical reasons of space.
The rented house in Oslo in which our Norwegian community
began its existence had a very small basement room available for
use as a chapel. Sisters gave us a large altar which had originally
been intended for a spacious convent chapel. Usually we
celebrated Mass with the sisters in their nearby convent, but the
three of us prayed the Offices together at home. There was no
possibility of anything other than very simple forms of
eucharistic adoration, since we had neither a thurible nor a large
and beautiful monstrance. After evening prayer each day, we
switched off the electric lights and left only two candles burning
on the altar and one lamp in front of the statue of Our Lady.
Incense was laid on a charcoal kindled on a small brazier. The
Blessed Sacrament was exposed in a small monstrance for fifteen
minutes of silent prayer, followed by a hymn and benediction.
Since our chapel was broader than it was long, the large altar
dominated it in such a way that we were all extremely close to the
host.

This was a new experience of prayer which we were able to
develop further when we moved to Molde, a small town on the

west coast of Norway, where our house-chapel was somewhat larger, and longer than it was broad. We placed the tabernacle directly in front of the one bay window. Next came the altar, which was large but not overwhelming, and on either side of it five chairs for the community and for the guests who came for retreats or quiet days of recollection. This half of the chapel was used during the Mass and the Offices. The other half was empty, with a carpet in neutral colours and a few chairs standing against the walls. This part of the chapel was used during eucharistic adoration.

After evening prayer each day, we moved from the chairs around the altar to the back half of the chapel. After one or two verses of a hymn, we switched off the electric lights. The chapel had such a low ceiling that even in the brightness of the Norwegian summer we noticed a clear difference in the amount of light. After some months, a sister came to live as a hermit in the house alongside our monastery. She joined us for most of our liturgical prayer, and since she was allergic to incense, we stopped using it – which made things even more simple. The Blessed Sacrament was exposed for half an hour of silent prayer, ending with benediction. It was too dark in the back half of the chapel to be able to read, so the eye had no external distractions from the act of looking at Jesus in the host, no more than two metres away from us.

I observed a variety of things going on, in myself and in the others present. There were usually four or five people in the chapel, but there might be two or even just myself. There was never any uniformity of physical posture. One might be kneeling on the carpet or on a prie-dieu, another sitting on a chair, another combining these positions by kneeling supported by a wooden prayer-stool. One Swedish guest adopted the lotus position. Almost all of those who took part felt it natural to prostrate themselves at full length on the ground. And almost all of us found ourselves falling asleep in this position! Sometimes out of physical tiredness, of course, but sometimes as a special grace from the same Lord who once said to his disciples, 'Come away and rest a while' (Mk 6:31). The floor of the chapel was not comfortable, but the physical act of lying face-downwards like a small child sleeping, secure because its mother is close at hand, made it easier to make the spiritual act of entrusting oneself wholly into the hands of the Lord – who often replied by giving us the gift of sleep.

Sleep itself may indeed be the direct answer to our prayer. A sister who visited us told me one morning that she had felt the pressure of so many problems that she could not sleep. So she went down to the chapel to bring all these problems to the Lord – 'And all of a sudden I woke up, and it was one o'clock!' She felt rather ashamed of herself for being so lax. I said: 'But wasn't the sleep God's reply to your anxieties?' Here, as always in the spiritual life, we must beware of being more pious than God! I have always liked the way St Poemen (d.c. 450) rebuked the other desert fathers who were scandalised when a young monk fell asleep during the long Offices: 'When I see one of my brothers sleeping in church, I take his head and place it on my knees.' One brother in Molde snored on occasion, but this was no more disturbing to the others than the tears which very often flowed during adoration.

Prayer during the time of exposition could be an utter desert, an anguished nothingness. Prayer could be a fountain of intercession that felt as if it was never going to stop flowing. Prayer could seem impossible because of all the problems that cried out for attention. Prayer could be unutterable joy, the union of love with Jesus. Prayer could be the gift of self-knowledge, taking the form of acute insight into hidden strata of sin and leading to despair ... or else to an act of confession on a much profounder level than ever before. The thirty minutes could drag by, or fly past. This taught me experientially the truth of something I knew on the theoretical level, namely that prayer is not something at my own disposal. We can indeed set aside time for prayer, but we cannot know whether there will in fact be any kind of prayer during that time. Prayer is God's gift to us, not primarily our gift to God.

When I entered the monastery, my cousin who was a Carmelite nun wrote to say, 'Your business now is to create peace for others. You may not experience very much of it yourself.' I remember a young man who visited our little community in Molde and surprised me by commenting on the atmosphere of peace he found there. He asked where this came from. I recalled my cousin's words from so many years before and told him, 'I think the peace comes because we try to expose ourselves to Christ's love.' I had in mind above all the eucharistic adoration in the house-chapel. The fruit of this was a peace that radiated out to others.

2

EXPOSED TO CHRIST

A 'power' went forth from Jesus
and healed those he encountered.
The same power radiates out
and heals us in our depths,
when we 'expose' ourselves
to the Christ who is 'exposed' to us in the eucharist.

It is unfortunate that English has merely taken over the Latin word *expositio* and given it the anglicised form 'exposition', for this is a technical ecclesiastical term existing within sacred precincts and never used by the English language in any other context ('Expo' comes from the French *exposition,* meaning 'exhibition'). The same Latin root gives us two other words, however, which belong very definitely outside the sanctuary: namely 'exposure' and 'exposed'. These words are vivid enough. They are used all the time in news broadcasts. Homeless people die of exposure on cold winter nights in our big cities, old people die of exposure as they flee from bombing raids. Exposure to a virus can afflict millions with influenza. And what are we 'exposed' to? Danger, risk, corrupting influences, temptation, infection, radiation (as happened after the accident at Chernobyl in 1986). We also use the term 'exposed' in relation to criminals and hypocrites or to an unsuspected connection between acts of wrongdoing. Is there any link between the sacred world of 'exposition' and the hazardous world of 'exposure' and 'exposed', any link that might reveal more deeply what it is we are doing when we adore the Christ who is 'exposed' in the sacrament?

I first sensed where the link might lie one evening in October 1981 in the church of St Gervais in Paris, which is entrusted to the religious Community of Jerusalem. There is exposition of the Blessed Sacrament in this church from Thursday evening until early on Friday morning every week, in a vigil that recalls Christ's solitary prayer in Gethsemane. At the end of the Mass, the hundreds of people present went in procession from the high altar to a side chapel, walking behind the priest who carried the host in a simple monstrance and one of the large pottery chalices containing the precious blood which had been consecrated during the Mass. The procession took a long time, with songs of praise and psalms and great clouds of incense filling the huge nave. The host and the chalice were then both placed on the side altar for adoration.

I remember thinking, 'But that is dangerous! The priest might drop the chalice ... or someone might bump into the altar, and the precious blood would be spilled.' And then it struck me that in reality, 'exposition' is not the colourless word our language has made it. Its true meaning is in fact 'exposure': exposure to risk. Was not the risk involved in carrying a full chalice in a lengthy procession and then setting it down, unprotected, on an altar actually a very eloquent image of the risk to which Jesus 'exposed' himself when he came among us as the messenger of the Father's love? The chalice risked having its contents spilled: was not this precisely the risk Jesus took by being faithful to his mission? And can we not say that he also takes a risk by letting himself be 'exposed' in the sacrament, the risk that we will reject his love today?

I then came to sense that there is a second kind of 'exposure' involved here too. Not only is Jesus exposed to us – by concentrating our gaze on Jesus in the host and opening ourselves to this personal encounter with him, *we expose ourselves to him, to the power that emanates from him now as it emanated while he was on earth.*

* * *

We hear about this power in general terms when Luke sets the scene for the Sermon on the Plain: 'And all in the crowd were trying to touch him, for power came out from him and healed all of them' (6:19), and in greater detail in Mark's account of the healing of a woman who suffered from haemorrhages (5:24ff.): 'A large crowd followed him and pressed in on him. Now there was a woman who had been suffering from haemorrhages for twelve years. She had endured much under many physicians, and had spent all that she had; and she was no better, but rather grew worse. She had heard about Jesus, and came up behind him in the crowd and touched his cloak, for she said, "If I but touch his clothes, I will be made well." Immediately her haemorrhage stopped, and she felt in her body that she was healed of her disease. *Immediately aware that power had gone forth from him,* Jesus turned about in the crowd and said, "Who touched my clothes?" And his disciples said to him, "You see the crowd pressing in on you; how can you say, 'Who touched me?'" He looked all around to see who had done it. But the woman, knowing what had happened to her, came in fear and trembling, fell down before him, and told him the whole truth. He said to her, "Daughter, your faith has made you well; go in peace, and be healed of your disease.'"

Matthew 9 and Luke 8 both shorten Mark's narrative. Matthew omits any mention of power going forth, but in Luke, after 'all deny it', Jesus himself tells Peter: 'Someone touched me; for *I noticed that power had gone out from me.'* These words make it clear that the woman is not healed through contact with some impersonal force radiating out from Jesus. He is not like the sun-lamp that alleviates rheumatic pain with its emanation of an impersonal warmth. His person is intimately involved.

But precisely because this is for him a personal encounter, Jesus cannot let the woman simply slip off into the anonymity of the crowd after she has been healed. He has exposed himself to her by allowing her to take hold of his cloak. Now she must dare to expose herself to him, for otherwise she would not advance beyond the initial level of faith, at which she believes that Jesus has the power to help her, to the deeper and decisive level at which faith means that the whole person responds in love to the person of Jesus. And that is the relationship Jesus wants with those whom he helps. Indeed, this is more than just a desire on his part: 'Christ has a clear *right* to meet all those whom he has redeemed, to meet each and every one of us,' as Pope John Paul II wrote in his first encyclical *Redemptor hominis* (1979, 20; my italics).

She takes the risk of exposing herself to Jesus: 'The woman fell down before him, and told him the whole truth.' She brings her own self to Jesus and tells how her illness had excluded her from religious society and ruined her economically. She tells him that no doctor could help, and that he was her only hope. Jesus had already healed these dimensions of her life when she touched his clothes and power went forth from him. Now she receives something else: she becomes a member of Jesus' family. This is why he calls her 'Daughter'. And her story provides us with a reliable image of what happens when we adore Christ in the eucharist.

* * *

In eucharistic adoration, we expose ourselves to Jesus in the same way as this woman. Like her, we hope for healing and expose our wounds to his life-giving power. And then, like her, we take the deeper risk of defencelessness, exposing our wounded selves and telling him the whole truth so that he can see us as we are, without any protective covering. Thus exposed, the woman experienced the transformation of her inner life: and our lives too can be transformed by Jesus.

The variety of experiences of prayer during eucharistic adoration which I mentioned in chapter 1, and the variety of physical reactions – especially tears and sleep – are signs that the power emanating from Jesus in the host is getting to work in us.

It is of course true that he does not always signalise his presence. His aim is to heal us in our depths, and this level is not always accessible to our own feelings or intellect. We may spend half an hour in prayer without feeling anything at all, and thinking only distracted thoughts, yet perhaps it is precisely in this half hour that the Lord touches us most profoundly. He says to Peter, 'You do not know now what I am doing, but later you will understand' (Jn 13:7). We should bear these words in mind when we reflect in general terms on our own spiritual biography, and in particular on the potential significance of what we experience or do not experience in prayer. We cannot make experience a criterion of closeness to God, and the Church has underlined this principle repeatedly in the past century by canonising a great number of saints who never had any special 'mystical graces' but who simply lived the life of faith – like us.

Having made this proviso, let us discuss one experience in prayer which can be extremely troubling. I compose myself in stillness to adore the Lord, but instead I find myself overwhelmed by sexual fantasies. Maybe I remember things I have done in the past, maybe images I have seen in films or advertising suddenly flash up on the internal screen of my mind, maybe I think about a specific person who kindles desire in me. Or else I find myself agitated by violent aggression. I remember things that specific persons have done against me or against those I love. I become bitter. I give way to feelings of hatred or revenge. All distractions take my attention away from Jesus, but these seem to do something much worse: they nullify my time of prayer by turning it into a time of sin. Evagrius of Pontus (d. 399), the supremely perceptive analyst of the spiritual path, said: 'One who loves true prayer and yet gives way to anger or resentment [in the time of prayer] is his own enemy. It is as if in the endeavour to see more clearly, one succeeded in fact only in inflicting damage on one's own eyes.' Surely, as a committed follower of Jesus, I ought not to be having such feelings?

What, then, is going on here? The light of Christ is falling on the whole of my being, and 'everything exposed by the light becomes visible' (Ep 5:13). In their context, these words speak of the 'unfruitful works of darkness'(5:10-11) which become visible to other people, but they can well be applied to this situation in which my own works of darkness become inescapably visible to my own self. Before Christ can heal me, I must become aware of what it is in me that needs to be healed! This is a painful discovery which usually begins in the dimension of sexuality, not because sexual sins are more serious *per se* than any others, but for two reasons: firstly, because sexuality is the area in which we most easily recognise our brokenness, our incapacity to love God, other people and our own selves; and, secondly, because we are all heirs to a Catholic moral tradition which has paid very great attention to questions of purity, so that we are sensitised in advance to the potential presence of sin here.

But the discovery of one's own aggressiveness *as sin* can be even more radically painful, because this dark dimension can so easily disguise itself. One can be consumed by ambition, greed for power and hatred of other people, while being wholly convinced that one is fighting the Lord's battles, and one would be horrified by the very suggestion that all this vigorous activity in the name of the Lord is merely promoting one's own agenda, be it a conservative one to preserve undiluted orthodoxy or a progressive one to defend the poor (however they are defined) against the mighty.

We are often told, and we may indeed be sincerely convinced, that there are tremendous gulfs separating the various groups in the Church, but this is to look too superficially at what is going on. C.S. Lewis' devil pointed out over fifty years ago in the *Screwtape Letters* that the powers of evil do not really care what instruments are employed to ensnare us, and we can perfectly well update what he wrote about the divisions in the Anglican Church then and apply it to the Catholic Church today. There is no difference from the vantage-point of hell between those who are effusively loyal to the Pope and those who are ferociously critical of him, between those who identify the Gospel with the overthrowing of oppressive structures in the Church and the world and those who identify the Gospel with the entrenching of such structures. All that matters is that we are on the devil's side, while all the time deluding ourselves that we are on God's side. Even causes that unite Catholics, such as the defence of unborn life, can be perverted so that there are some in our Church who defend acts of physical aggression against abortion clinics and their personnel in supposed support of the sanctity of life, though violence 'in the name of Jesus' is a contradiction in terms. As he said in Gethsemane when Peter wanted to defend him by violence: 'Put your sword back into its place; for all who take the sword will perish by the sword' (Mt 26:52).

The discovery, under the irradiation of Christ's love from the host, that our unilluminated aggression has taken us so far from his path, usually comes at a later stage in life than the discovery that we need to be healed by him in the realm of our sexuality. This is because our spiritual biography has phases corresponding to our human biography in general. At twenty-five, the Christian will have some experience of what human sexuality is, though not yet of what it means in sexual terms (for example) to have been married to the same person for twenty years, or to be abandoned by one's partner, or to be forty-five and deeply lonely; correspondingly, the terrible experience of what one's own sin can mean in this fundamentally important dimension of human existence deepens with time. Even more so, the young Christian cannot yet have had enough experience of what the yearning for power and the actual exercise of power genuinely mean in human life to be able to assess the tragedy – and the sheer wickedness – of the Christian misuse of the aggressive instinct (which in itself is a good gift from God). This takes time. It cannot be rushed, by myself or by a spiritual counsellor, for otherwise I would never get beyond the stage of an intellectual assent to a *theory* about sin.

This is why the discovery of my real sinfulness (and not just of my individual sinful acts) presupposes that I have lived a good number of years; the longer I live, the deeper my discovery can go. It is a great grace of the Lord when the tectonic plates of my existence shift before my inner eye, and he lets me see how much of my life, under a lovely veneer of piety and goodness, is in fact sin and atheism. To accept this is humbling – and leads to the grace of healing.

Pope John Paul II has invited the Church to repent of past misdeeds as a penitential preparation for the year 2000: 'The Church should become more fully conscious of the sinfulness of her children, recalling all those times in history when they departed from the spirit of Christ and his Gospel and, instead of offering to the world the witness of a life inspired by the values of faith, indulged in ways of thinking and acting which were truly *forms of counter-witness and scandal*' (Apostolic Letter *Tertio millennio adveniente*, 1994, 33). This is salutary, but the danger is that we could limit ourselves to a cheap polemic – cheap, because we would draw up a list of the well-known and indefensible past and present crimes of the Church (the Crusades, the Inquisition, the shady goings-on of the Vatican Bank and so on) but pass by the much more costly confession of our own personal 'unfruitful works of darkness'. Exposure to Christ's light gives me the possibility of genuinely admitting what lies in my heart – admitting this to myself in the act of insight, but simultaneously to him in the act of confession.

Those who confessed their sins to Jesus were pardoned. The woman caught in the act of adultery did not try to deny the fact of what she had done, or to redefine it as no sin at all but rather the expression of a sincere interpersonal love. She just remained standing exposed before Jesus, who then said: 'I do not condemn you' (Jn 8:11). The same is true of us, and this is why the insight into our sinfulness should never make us give up in despair. Our exposure to Christ in eucharistic adoration can often lead us to the sacrament of confession in which we receive Christ's forgiveness.

How then should I react to severe temptations to aggression or lust during prayer? I should try to confront these with a good portion of serenity, for they are in fact a sign of progress in the spiritual life. They mean that the Lord is getting to work at a deeper level in me, stirring up the placid waters of my piety to get down to the mud in my heart. If I do not flinch from the pain, I will find that the power emanating from him heals me in my depths, in a lifelong process that configures me more and more to Christ.

3

PRACTICAL SUGGESTIONS

I can sum up the previous two chapters by saying that in all these different ways, what we experience in adoration is the Lord's power. The reflections in the second part of this book attempt to penetrate more deeply into individual dimensions of this encounter with Christ as an answer to potential objections. Their aim is always practical, to share an experience and encourage others. Hence I conclude the first part with some simple suggestions.

It goes without saying that not everyone can have the concrete possibility of praying in this way. The increasing shortage of priests in the active ministry means that many pastors are already totally overburdened, so that they may well react with scepticism to the suggestion that they practise eucharistic adoration on top of everything else; and very many committed lay people are equally overburdened by the demands society makes on them in their family life and their work, so that these pages may seem far removed from reality.

I do not want in any way to suggest that everyone must incorporate this into the life of prayer; the only prayer that has ever been seen as obligatory for all is the Sunday liturgy. All I want is to suggest that the Church has a very rich spiritual treasure here, especially as this has developed in the decades after the Second Vatican Council, and that we ought not to overestimate the practical difficulties. The declericalisation of eucharistic adoration which I mentioned in the Introduction opens doors that could lead to an enrichment of many people's love for Jesus Christ. And, as I shall attempt to show, that love is the very heart of the Christian existence.

* * *

The school chapel where I used to go to Mass had an altar frontal on which were embroidered the words: *Magister adest et vocat te*, 'The Master is here and is calling you'. These words come from St John's Gospel (11:28): they are spoken by Martha in Bethany, when she calls her sister Mary to come and meet Jesus. The frontal applied them to the tabernacle above the altar, addressing them to those who came into the chapel, and they supply the title for this book. What then should we do, when we answer his call and come into his presence?

For the individual's prayer, the classic advice is given by Abbot John Chapman of Downside (d.1933) in one of his letters: 'Pray as you can, not as you can't.' Each of us must take this freedom seriously.

The tradition of the Church and the continuing creativity of the Holy Spirit in our own days offer us an immense wealth of experience on which to draw when we pray; but all attempts at a standardisation of the spiritual life, every insistence that we are obliged to pray in one specific way, must be rejected as fatal misunderstandings. Those who assert that they have received private revelations often claim that Jesus or Mary commands *everyone* to practise certain forms of piety; for example, as I write, the newspapers here in Munich report the claim of a local priest that God the Father has made known to one of his parishioners the heavenly wish that everyone should pray the entire fifteen mysteries of the Rosary every day. In order to set a good example, we are told, this lady herself prays no less than fourteen Rosaries, i.e. fourteen times the entire fifteen mysteries, every day. Such things belong (along with ascetic feats of the past like the desert monk who ate only five dried figs in the course of a whole week) more to the realm of the *Guinness Book of Records* than to the Christian religion, which frees us forever from all such prescriptions: 'Do not let anyone condemn you in matters of food and drink or of observing festivals, new moons, or sabbaths. These are only a shadow of what is to come, but the substance belongs to Christ. Do not let anyone disqualify you, insisting on self-abasement and worship of angels ...' (Col 2:16ff.). 'For freedom Christ has set us free. Stand firm, therefore, and do not submit again to a yoke of slavery' (Ga 5:1).

The Christian can therefore pray in whatever way is found

natural and helpful. I offer, only as a suggestion, some short scriptural prayers which I have often found coming into my mind in the presence of Christ exposed in the host. I have repeated them over and over again, in the same way as one repeats the Jesus Prayer. They can help to concentrate our attention on the Lord, when we find our thoughts wandering too far away.

- 'Lord, it is good that we are here' (Mt 17:4, Peter's words when Jesus is transfigured)
- 'Increase our faith!' (Lk 17:5)
- 'Lord, heal my soul, for I have sinned against you' (Ps 41:4)
- 'The Lord is my shepherd, there is nothing I shall want' (Ps 23:1)
- 'With you is the fountain of life; in your light we see light' (Ps 36:9)
- 'The Lord is my light and my salvation; whom shall I fear?' (Ps 27:1)

* * *

Let me offer some suggestions about eucharistic adoration in common. First, it is important that those taking part know in advance what the group is going to do. 'God is a God not of disorder but of peace' (1 Co 14:33), and this means that it is good to have a simple structure to which the group becomes accustomed. This applies to the beginning and to the close of the prayer, which should always have the same pattern.

The group begins its adoration with a short reading from scripture (for example, the Gospel from the liturgy of the day) and/or with a song or hymn in which all can join. After this comes silent prayer.

The beginning is important because a Christian cannot just 'snap into' an activity like prayer. And this is because the Christian is a human being and is subject to the ordinary psychological laws governing human conduct. The players at Wimbledon do not just snap into the activity of tennis, the actors in a theatre do not just snap into the activity of playing their roles. There is a necessary psychological threshold that must be crossed first, and since we exist in the dimension of time, this means that the tennis players and the actors have to *take time* to prepare and then execute this transition from their everyday activity to their highly demanding professional activity. In the case of the liturgy, however – which believers claim is the highest of all human activities – we see a completely different attitude at work. In Catholic churches all over the world, the congregation is thin on the ground five minutes before the Mass begins and much more populous by the time the Gospel is read. This is the bad fruit of a legalistic moral theology that – like so much Catholic moral theology – concentrated on the fulfilment of laws (How late can I come to the service and still satisfy the obligation of attending Mass on Sunday?) and ignored the psychological reality of what it is to be a human being. To arrive late for Mass (except, obviously, in unavoidable situations) and still expect to get spiritual fruit out of the liturgical prayer is to put God to the test by asking him to hop over precisely this psychological reality which he himself created.

In the case of group prayer, this means that the members arrive a little while before the beginning, so that there is time (if necessary) to rehearse the music and allocate particular tasks, and each one can come to the external silence without which there is no access to internal silence.

Silent prayer means literally that: silent prayer. Background music on a CD or a cassette is an escape-route from the exposure to Christ of which I spoke in chapter 2, because it clothes our nakedness by giving the ear something to feed on. I do not underestimate the difficulty of this kind of desert silence. None of us finds it easy. But if we hold out, without running away, then we shall experience how 'the wilderness and the dry land shall be glad, the desert shall rejoice and blossom ... the burning sand shall become a pool, and the thirsty ground springs of water' (Is 35).

A group can experiment to see what duration is appropriate to them; an hour is probably the absolute maximum for a group, though an individual praying alone might sometimes feel called to pray longer. It is important that everyone knows how long the silent prayer will last, and that there is an agreed way of ending it. This might be another song, or freely formulated prayers of intercession; or one person might read the invocations of a litany while the others respond with 'Have mercy on us'. If a priest or deacon is present, he can give benediction before putting the Blessed Sacrament back into the tabernacle. After this, the group could for example pray Compline together, or a decade of the Rosary. Since these both involve many words, they can function as a helpful transition back to everyday activity – one cannot just snap out of intense prayer any more than one can just snap into it!

It is important to pay attention to the physical setting. I think it is valuable to switch off all the electric lights and have only a few candles burning near the monstrance, as we did in Norway. This concentrates the eye very effectively. No one should be too far away from the altar, though one can of course increase the visibility by using an extra-large host for adoration. The space available sets limits on the size of the group, since each person should have enough space to take up the posture that is best for prayer, and should also be able to change this posture in the course of the period of adoration without disturbing the others by breathing down their neck or butting them in the back. In practice, this means that the chapel or room used should have a minimum of furniture. Church benches are a straitjacket that unnecessarily constricts this kind of group prayer; the requirements here are not at all the same as for the celebration of the parish Mass or for exposition on the main altar of a large church in the presence of a congregation.

Incense and flowers allow the sense of smell to worship God. They can be a great contribution to prayer, but they may irritate some individuals (as we found in Norway), so the group must agree on how much to use. Irrespective of whether or not strong fragrances are used, it is useful to keep a window open, so that some fresh air may circulate. Here too, of course, the group is called to exercise mutual consideration.

A final, very important point: I often had to reassure people who jumped up from prayer in the chapel in Molde when they heard the telephone ringing, and looked surprised and even reproachful when I did not run out to answer it, that we had an answering machine and that I would hear any messages later on. By now, answering machines are much more commonplace, and if the adoration is taking place in a house-chapel or some other private room where the group could be disturbed by the telephone, then the machine should be switched on for the duration of adoration. Unless a doctor on call is present, mobile telephones must be switched off. Bleeping wrist-watches seem to have gone out of fashion, but those who still have them should leave them outside the door!

PART TWO

POTENTIAL OBJECTIONS

4

THREE QUESTIONS

1. A divisive prayer?

I wrote in chapter 2 that things which are very good *per se* (such as the defence of unborn life) can be perverted so that they divide believers instead of uniting them. The same can be true of eucharistic adoration.

I have often suggested to religious communities, in the course of retreats I have given, that they should try to discover for themselves some of the riches of silent eucharistic adoration, by making available to the individual members the possibility of this kind of prayer at some regular point in the week or indeed each day, only to hear the objection that this would divide the community into those who took part (and disparaged the others as worldly) and those who did not take part (and disparaged the others as 'holier than thou'). This potential problem is then resolved either by never having eucharistic adoration or else by imposing it on the whole community. The second alternative brings us back to the situation I experienced in my own monastery, where adoration was merely one point on the spiritual programme, something that took no account of the inclinations and the varying spiritual needs of the individuals involved.

The point of my suggestion is not that communities should shoulder yet another burden. The point is that the contemporary flowering of silent adoration offers each member a specific possibility of growing in the love of Jesus Christ. How then can the freedom of the individual be respected in such a way that divisions are avoided?

The answer is found in Paul's counsel to the Romans, who were divided by similar problems: 'Some judge one day [i.e. the sabbath] to be better than another, while others judge all days to be alike. Let all be fully convinced in their own minds. Those who observe the day, observe it in honour of the Lord. Also those who eat, eat in honour of the Lord, since they give thanks to

God; while those who abstain, abstain in honour of the Lord and give thanks to God.' And he warns them: 'Let us no longer pass judgement on one another' because of divergent spiritual practices (14:5ff.). Utopian? Well, possibly – but only in the sense that the whole Christian project is Utopian. And we are not entitled to dismiss the Gospel, or even to water it down, just because it sets us such a demanding standard!

This can be an exercise in ecumenism, the process of growth in unity which must take place continuously, not only between the Churches, but also within the Catholic Church itself. Accepting that the Spirit calls each of us to take a particular path within the rich diversity of the fellowship of the Church as a whole, or within the specific fellowship of one religious community or parish, and that our faithfulness to this particular path will in fact enrich the whole fellowship rather than imperil it, demands a human and spiritual maturity which is itself a gift of the Spirit of God, a gift for which we must pray. For without this serenity and mutual acceptance, there will never be any genuine unity within the Church, let alone between the Churches.

We must be realistic here, for the difficulties are not to be brushed aside as if they were merely potential problems. It is a matter of observable fact, in the years after the Council, that tremendous tensions have been introduced into a number of religious communities by the demands of individuals or of groups that they be allowed to follow a particular spirituality (the charismatic renewal, Focolare, Opus Angelorum ...), and into a number of parishes by groups such as the Neocatechumenate. I use the neutral word 'tensions' deliberately! Tensions in the Church can be a sign of growth; they can equally be a sign of disintegration. Deciding precisely what is indicated by specific tensions is a task calling for great gifts of discernment. It may thus be the case that, in particular circumstances, we judge that it is better – at least for the moment – to renounce the potential spiritual enrichment which eucharistic adoration would bring.

At the same time, we must not overestimate the difficulties. For, as Saying 109 in the second-century Gospel of Philip so marvellously puts it, 'When the Holy Spirit blows, the summer comes'. One of the ways in which the Spirit blows in our day is through the renewed practice of the adoration of Jesus exposed in the sacrament of the altar. We must trust that, where tensions and misunderstandings arise, the Spirit will also give us the wisdom and strength, and above all the mutual Christian love, to put into practice Paul's counsel in Romans 14.

*   *   *

2. Is it truly justifiable to look at the host?

It is a matter of historical fact that the elevation of the host (and later of the chalice) at the consecration in the Mass, and exposition and processions of the Blessed Sacrament, were introduced at a period when lay people received communion very seldom. Their deepest wish was to share in the mystery of the eucharist, not by receiving the sacrament, but *by seeing Jesus as directly as possible.* Special stipends were sometimes paid to priests in return for an extended elevation of the Host.

Things change in the history of spirituality, and the desire to receive the sacrament has grown in intensity until, thanks above all to the decrees of St Pius X (d.1914), it has become normal for those who take part in the celebration of the Mass to receive the Body of Christ. Severe fasting rules have been progressively relaxed until only a symbolic remnant is left; there is a feeling of being in a wholly different world when one reads (for example) the narrative of the Jesuit Michel d'Herbigny's mission to communist Russia in 1926, when Pius XI sent him to establish a secret hierarchy by ordaining bishops. He met two young Catholic men who had not seen a priest for years and had therefore had no opportunity to receive the sacraments, but although he was in fact carrying the host in a pyx on his person, he could not give them communion, since they had known nothing of his journey and had already eaten that day!

Not only have all such restrictions been swept away; the Second Vatican Council also took the first steps to reintroduce communion from the chalice, so that the Lord's solemn commandment – 'Take, eat, this is my body... Drink from it, all of you; for this is my blood of the covenant' (Mt 26:27f.) – is obeyed today with a frequency unparalleled in Church history.

This is certainly one of the most dramatic and fruitful examples of the Holy Spirit's renewal of the Church in the twentieth century.

And so it has often been implied, or asserted openly, that exposition and adoration have become an obsolete practice, since their function as a *de facto* substitute for holy communion is no longer required. Indeed, a further question is asked: is it justifiable at all to look at a sacrament which was instituted to be eaten (and drunk)?

This is to think much too functionally about the spiritual life. Jesus came, not only to give us life – that is, to satisfy the primary needs we do in fact have in our relationship to God, such as nourishment – but to give life 'abundantly' (Jn 10:10), that is, to give us far more than is strictly necessary. His first sign at Cana symbolises this (Jn 2:1ff.). The wedding guests are already drunk, so we cannot speak of a situation of genuine need when Jesus turns an enormous quantity of water into wine. It is not in the least comparable to the distress of the five thousand in the wilderness for whom he multiplies the loaves and fishes. There is almost something playful about this seemingly unnecessary first miracle, though the playfulness has a serious message: the 'glory Jesus revealed' (Jn 2:12) at Cana was the glory of the one who gives superabundantly, without any limitation other than the recipients' capacity to grasp what he is giving them.

We could therefore take a very long historical view over the whole of the second Christian millennium as it draws to its close, and see the introduction of eucharistic devotion in the Middle Ages and its continuation today as one example of this superabundant gift the Lord makes – not merely 'life', but 'life to the full'.

This is true, but there is another aspect still to be considered: namely, love's desire to see Jesus as directly as is possible here on earth. The eye finds nourishment in the celebration of the Mass; but at the same time, the liturgy intends to nourish all the other senses, since it is in the highest degree a bodily action. And what our body does here has eternal consequences: St Irenaeus of Lyons (d.202) says that precisely because our mortal flesh has received the flesh of the Son of God in the eucharist, our

Christian hope is not merely the immortality of the soul, but the resurrection of the body.

No act of worship is higher than the celebration of the Mass. But the liturgy cannot be allowed to exist in isolation, as if it could satisfy all our legitimate spiritual needs and aspirations. The requirement that we preserve the unity of the liturgical action *as an action* means that we cannot devote too much time or attention to any one particular element in the celebration, and this principle entails that no single one of our senses is going to find its full spiritual nourishment in the Mass. For example, we do move around a little in the liturgy, when we leave our seats and go forward to receive communion and come back, and in the offertory procession, or on special occasions like Palm Sunday and the veneration of the Cross on Good Friday; but the feet need and want more, and this is why we have devotions like the Stations of the Cross in our churches and why people go on pilgrimages. Similarly, the eye needs and wants more than it can find in the liturgy alone. We can see Christ in an icon which mediates his presence to our prayer. But we can see him, less pictorially but infinitely more directly, in eucharistic adoration, where the eyes of the flesh see the host in the monstrance while the eyes of faith see the Master and contemplate him in love.

To reject this desire of our eye, and say that it must be content with what it finds in the celebration of the liturgy, is the sign of a puritanism which refuses to take human bodiliness – and the incarnation of God as the redemption and sanctification of this bodiliness – with full seriousness.

* * *

3. Is prayer to the Son really legitimate?
Jesus says: 'Whoever sees me sees him who sent me'; 'Whoever has seen me has seen the Father' (Jn 12:45; 14:9). Thus, the eyes of faith are meant to recognise a transparency in Jesus. Although he puts his own person at the very heart of his preaching, crying out, 'Come to me!' (Mt 11:28), 'Let anyone who is thirsty come to me!' (Jn 7:37), the reason he wants to attract people to himself is that he is 'the way' to the Father (Jn 14:6). He says, 'I do not

seek my own glory' (Jn 8:50); in everything he does, he 'seeks the glory of the one who sent him' (Jn 7:18). Does this mean that our love should be directed to the Father, and that it is wrong to speak of loving Jesus, as I have done at such length?

There is a recurrent temptation in the history of Christianity to try to dispense with Jesus' mediation to us of the Father's love. This temptation takes different forms, generated by the theological reasonings at work in such very different spheres as the East Syriac mysticism of the eighth century or the spiritual authors against whom St Teresa of Avila reacted in the sixteenth. When this temptation occurs in our own century, it is usually linked to a reluctance (more or less explicit) to accept the divinity of Jesus: for if he is not God, he cannot be an object of prayer or of love in the same way as the Father. We sometimes hear the objection that prayer to Jesus cannot be legitimate, since he himself prayed to the Father – and the Christian must be one who follows Jesus' example! This is one of the main accusations made against the Christian Churches by Jehovah's Witnesses, who claim to be faithful to the teaching of Jesus in the Gospels.

This is obviously true in a wooden, literal sense. Jesus did not pray to himself! But the New Testament shows Christians praying to Jesus from the very beginning. I refer for the sake of brevity only to two significant texts:

• Stephen has a vision of 'the heavens opened and the Son of Man standing at the right hand of God', and cries out as he dies: '*Lord Jesus,* receive my spirit!' (Acts 7:55ff.). This prayer of the first martyr is based on Psalm 31:5, quoted by Jesus on the Cross (see Lk 23:46), which says to Yahweh: 'Into your hands I commit my spirit.'

• The last words of the New Testament are an affirmation about Jesus, an invocation of Jesus and a blessing in his name: 'The one who testifies to these things says, "Surely I am coming soon." Amen. *Come, Lord Jesus!* The grace of the Lord Jesus be with all the saints. Amen' (Rv 22:20f.). The same prayer is found in Aramaic at 1 Corinthians 16:21 and in chapter 9 of the Didache in a liturgical text which goes back to the first century: *Maranatha!*

The testimony of scripture and of the entire tradition of the

Church is that one cannot go behind the Son, as it were, in order to get more directly to the Father. There is quite simply no access to the Father for us other than in our relationship to the living person of Jesus: 'I am the way, and the truth, and the life. No one comes to the Father except through me. If you know me, you will know my Father also' (Jn 14:6f.). The doctrine of the Trinity is the absolutely fundamental structure of the Christian revelation of God, that which distinguishes Christianity from the other two great religions with a semitic origin, Judaism and Islam. And this doctrine entails that even when we see God 'face to face' in heaven (to borrow Paul's expression in 1 Corinthians 13:12), it will still be Jesus who mediates this vision to us. Since it is Jesus' love that is the mediation of the Father's love for us, our love for the Father cannot bypass him, either here on earth or in eternity.

This is why the Johannine writings, the Gospel and the Letters, can speak quite unsystematically of the Father's love for us and Jesus' love for us, of our love for the Father and our love for Jesus, without apparently feeling any need to tidy up their vocabulary.

This is also the reason why it is unimportant whether we pray to the Father, to the Son, or to the Holy Spirit when we address God. Our prayer is always a participation through the Holy Spirit in the eternal dynamic of the dialogue of love between the Father and the Son. This is the unceasing movement whereby the Father and the Son eternally give themselves to one another and receive themselves back – and give themselves anew. The Persons of the Trinity hold back nothing for their own selves. Thus the love for Jesus which we express in our prayer is always drawn by the Spirit into the Son's own love for the Father, so that we will have a deeper love for the Father; and the love for the Father which we express in our prayer is always drawn by the Spirit into the Father's love for the Son, so that we will have a deeper love for Jesus. And since the Spirit is their mutual love, invoking the Spirit will likewise lead us more deeply into the mystery of the Trinity, which is not some object of abstruse theological speculations, but is the reality which dwells in us now and which we shall adore for all eternity, as Blessed Elizabeth of the Trinity (d.1906) put it in her famous prayer: 'O my God, Trinity whom

I adore ... bury yourself in me so that I may bury myself in you, while I wait for the day when I shall depart to contemplate the abyss of your greatness in your light.'

This means that an expression of personal love for Jesus Christ such as eucharistic adoration is a perfectly legitimate form of Christian prayer. It also means that the Jesus whom the eyes of faith see in the host is transparent to the Father, so that we can bear in mind here too his words to Philip: 'Whoever has seen me has seen the Father' (Jn 14:9).

5

IS LOVE FOR JESUS TRULY SO CENTRAL?

> Eucharistic adoration is an encounter with the living Lord
> which makes sense only as an encounter of mutual love.
> This love is the central dimension of the Christian life:
> the Christian is one who receives the love of Jesus
> with its radical demands,
> and who loves him in return.

Referring to relationships among Christians, Ian Paisley wrote many years ago in his in his commentary on the Letter to the Romans that truth was more important than love; many in all the Christian denominations would agree with him, even if perhaps few would care to say so. The same seems to apply to our relationship to the Lord: in practice, all the denominations give priority to orthodoxy, i.e. to believing the right things about Jesus, rather than to loving him. (For example, while there was a professor of spiritual theology in the faculty where I taught, he was very definitely subordinate to the professor of dogmatics!) This is presumably because it is much easier to assess the degree of orthodoxy in another person than to assess to the extent to which he or she loves the Lord.

I do not intend to question the importance of orthodoxy; history supplies plenty of examples of a deep emotional love for Jesus that cries out for theological enlightenment, such as the wondrous hymns in the fourth-century Manichaean Psalter or the writings of a number of mystically gifted Christians in our own century. Right faith is a necessity, not a luxury. But we must beware of putting the cart before the horse! The New Testament emphasises that one must believe aright: 'Everyone who does not abide in the teaching of Christ, but goes beyond it, does not have God; whoever abides in the teaching has both the Father and the Son' (2 Jn 9), but it warns with biting irony against mere orthodoxy:

'You believe that God is one; you do well. Even the demons believe – and shudder' (Jn 2:19).

Right faith can lead to gratitude – I accept the truth of what the Lord is and I give thanks for all he has done for me – but by itself, it cannot get beyond this threshold; as we so often see in human relationships, there is no necessary progression from gratitude to love. But if I locate my starting-point in the love of the Lord, then I find that this love spurs me on to discover more and more about him, a process which necessarily involves letting my faith be purified by contact with the living tradition of his Church. In other words, my concern for orthodoxy must be the fruit of love: it is because I have come to know the Lord's love for me, and I love him in return, that I wish to hold the right faith about him.

The silent prayer of eucharistic adoration makes sense *only* as an encounter of personal love between Jesus Christ and the Christian. One can perfectly well argue that it is useful (for many reasons) to read the Bible. One can argue that it is useful (again, for many reasons) to take part in the celebration of the Mass, and I remember that it was somewhat fashionable twenty-five years ago to come out of church and tell one another how helpful the service had been. We are also told that it is useful to pray the Divine Office (Paul VI urged that it makes one familiar with scripture, Cardinal John Heenan of Westminster wrote that it was like the five-finger exercises that prepare pianists for playing 'real' music). No doubt all of this is true, but it surely misses the point: the only motivation for prayer that will genuinely inspire us and sustain us in dry periods is love. For example, the first words John Paul II said to his secretary when he regained consciousness after the attack on his life in May 1981 were: 'Did we pray Compline yesterday?' That was surely the expression of a love for prayer, rather than of the mere conviction that it is useful to pray!

Be that as it may: silent eucharistic adoration has no observable function, no usefulness. It certainly bears fruit in the Christian life, indeed endlessly rich fruit – but only if it is carried out according to the logic of love. And love does not ask: 'What am I getting out of this?'

People who love each other want to spend time together. Nothing is more urgent or important for them than simply giving each other the most precious thing they possess, namely their time. An outsider may well consider this a waste of their time, but it appears eminently reasonable to them. In precisely the same way, the best thing we have to give Jesus, if we love him, is our time – and that is what we are doing in eucharistic adoration.

Where this love is lacking, adoration is bound to appear to be a waste of time that could be spent better, just as some thought the costly ointment was being wasted when the woman poured it over Jesus' head in the house of Simon the leper (Mk 14:3f.). But the woman was acting according to the logic of love, and Jesus defends her in extraordinary words: 'Let her alone; why do you trouble her? She has performed a good service for me ... Truly I tell you, wherever the good news is proclaimed in the whole world, what she has done will be told in remembrance of her.' Why is this unnamed woman to be an integral part of the proclamation of the Gospel in the whole world – something Jesus never says about anyone else? Surely, because she alone has grasped the centrality of the love that (in St Ignatius' words) gives without counting the cost.

It is therefore important to establish whether the kind of priority that eucharistic adoration gives to the encounter of personal love corresponds to what the Gospels have to tell us about the Master. What is the best way, then, to describe the relationship between Jesus and his disciples – the relationship into which he calls us to enter?

*   *   *

The New Testament often says that Jesus gave his life out of love for us: 'We know love by this, that he laid down his life for us' (1 Jn 3:16); 'Christ loved us and gave himself up for us, a fragrant offering and sacrifice to God' (Ep 5:2). This is not just a love *en masse*, so to speak, a designation of Jesus' relationship to the totality of humanity or of the Church. Paul can speak here of a personal love that has him in view: 'I live by faith in the Son of God, who loved me and gave himself for me' (Ga 2:20).

The Fourth Gospel likewise speaks of this sacrificial love: 'No one has greater love than this, to lay down one's life for one's friends. You are my friends ...' (15:13f.). But it also tells us of Jesus' love during his ministry, thereby supplying a reliable image, a significant pattern of his abiding relationship to his disciples. Far more than a mere biographical detail is involved when John speaks of 'the disciple whom Jesus loved'. He reclines on Jesus' breast at the Last Supper, he stands faithfully under the Cross when the other male disciples have fled in fear, and he is the first of these male disciples to come to the tomb on Easter morning and to recognise the risen Jesus by the Sea of Galilee. Who is he? Tradition identifies him with John the son of Zebedee, while modern scholarship doubts this; but perhaps the very fact that his name is not given is itself significant, for it opens up a suggestive path. If we leave the historical question of his identity aside here, can we not see him as one of the reliable images of scripture which show us how God acts today? The figure who is given no name or title other than 'the disciple whom Jesus loved' would thus be the embodiment of what it is to be a follower of Jesus. In other words, *everyone* whom Jesus calls, and who responds to this call, becomes 'the disciple whom Jesus loves'. The specific vocation each one may have in the common task of building up the kingdom of God is secondary: the primary identity of each one is to be 'the disciple whom Jesus loves'.

This is confirmed by a vocational narrative in Mark 10: 'As he was setting out on a journey, a man ran up and knelt before him, and asked him, 'Good Teacher, what must I do to inherit eternal life?' ... "You know the commandments,"' says Jesus, and when the man asks for something more, Jesus gives him a very specific charge: 'You lack one thing; go, sell what you own, and give the money to the poor, and you will have treasure in heaven; then come, follow me.' This is the same invitation, or perhaps more accurately the summons, Jesus makes to Simon and Andrew in chapter 1 of Mark and to Levi in chapter 2. But here we have an important detail: 'Jesus, looking at him, *loved him* and said: "You lack one thing ..."' (10:21). The specific charge is thus rooted in Jesus' love for this man. His *primary vocation* was the invitation to accept this love, to let himself become 'the disciple whom Jesus loved' – and only then, as a consequence of this, to live this new identity in giving everything he owned to the poor and following Jesus on the roads of Galilee.

As we know, the rich man's heart was already occupied; he had no space to accept Jesus' love. But he too provides a reliable image, a significant pattern of how Jesus acts 'yesterday and today and forever'. What is said of him applies to ourselves. The encounter with Jesus is always an encounter with the entirely personal love he offers, an encounter with the potential to transform our lives – if we accept his love. So much is this the case that one of the medieval Cistercian mystics, St Mechthild of Hackeborn (d.1299), can put these words on the lips of the Lord: 'When Judas kissed me, my heart felt such love that – had he but repented – I would have made his soul my bride, thanks to that kiss.'

Thus every one of us can say that we have been called by Jesus in love. And this experience of being loved by him – of accepting our identity as 'the beloved disciple' – is the abiding and ever-renewed basis of our love for him, which will then take the concrete forms in our individual lives which he determines. Without this fundamental experience of being loved by Jesus and being served by him, of having one's feet washed by him – it is impossible for us to love him and serve him, as the earliest Christian poet (in the mid-second century) recognised:

> I would not have known how to love the Lord,
> had he not loved me;
> who is able to discern love,
> except the one who is loved? (Odes of Solomon 3:4f.)

And once we have indeed recognised and accepted his love, we cannot do anything other than love him, for this is the logic of love, expressed with unsurpassable concision sixteen hundred years later than the Odes of Solomon by Filippo Bruni in his hymn for the feast of the Sacred Heart: *Quis non amantem redamet?* Who could fail to love in return him who loves?

* * *

We see the centrality of this love for the person of Jesus in the story of his forgiveness of Peter after the resurrection. Peter's threefold denial was not some superficial act that left his relationship to Jesus substantially intact (what moral theologians have called a 'venial sin'). It lay on a much deeper level of his being, as a failure to give the appropriate response of love to Jesus' love for him (the response which the 'beloved disciple' and the women under the Cross had given). Peter realised this – but so did Jesus. Luke tells us: 'At that moment, while he was still speaking, the cock crowed. *The Lord turned and looked at Peter.* Then Peter remembered the word of the Lord, how he had said to him, "Before the cock crows today, you will deny me three times." And he went out and wept bitterly' (22:60ff.). The words I have italicised are enigmatic in the sense that they do not spell out in psychological detail what this betrayal meant for the relationship between Jesus and Peter, but they are clear enough. Luke, unlike the other evangelists, wants us to know that Jesus was fully aware of Peter's denial.

John 21:15ff. shows us how Jesus, after his resurrection, takes the initiative to restore the relationship. All he does is to ask one question, but he asks it three times in keeping with Peter's threefold denial: 'Do you love me?'

'The one to whom little has been forgiven, loves little,' said Jesus (Lk 7:47). Peter has been forgiven something very serious, and his realisation of the depth of his sin and of the depth of Jesus' forgiveness calls forth in him a new depth of love for Jesus, the love which will make him lead Jesus' sheep to pasture, and finally follow the Master even to death.

In John 21 Peter gives us a reliable image, a significant pattern which can be set alongside the story of the rich man in Mark 10. Discipleship thus means love on both sides, a truly mutual relationship: 'Those who have my commandments and keep them are *those who love me,* and those who love me will be loved by my Father, and *I will love them* and reveal myself to them' (Jn 14:21).

* * *

45

We should note that this is something completely new, without any precedents in Judaism. Jews at the time of Jesus recited words from Deuteronomy three times a day: 'Hear, O Israel: The Lord is our God, the Lord alone. You shall love the Lord your God with all your heart, and with all your soul, and with all your might ...' (6:4f.). Jesus himself identifies this as the first commandment (Mk 12:29). When the New Testament talks about loving God, therefore, it is not saying anything new.

The new element is love for the person of the Messiah. Many Jewish texts of the period between the Old Testament and the New speak of how God would intervene in history to set his people free; not all looked for an anointed king from the house of David, but many Jews had this hope. None of these texts ever speaks of loving the Messiah. He is never called the bridegroom of Israel, and the individual member of the Jewish people is never exhorted to love him. It is the impact of Jesus' person that has brought in something completely new here, something that the first Christians saw as an essential mode of expressing their relationship to Jesus.

Two texts show us that 'essential' is the correct term here. In the farewell discourses of John, Jesus divides the human race into two categories: 'Those who love me will keep my word ... whoever does not love me does not keep my words' (14:23f.). What is at stake here is not whether people accept or reject Jesus' teaching, whether they acknowledge or dismiss his miracles as evidence that he is the Messiah whom the Father has sent. For it is perfectly possible to discuss such questions in a spirit of academic detachment that insulates the debaters from confrontation with the real issue – which is always existential! The classic example of this detachment in the New Testament is Paul's Athenian audience: 'Now all the Athenians and the foreigners living there would spend their time in nothing but telling or hearing something new', writes Luke, and when they hear Paul speak about the resurrection they simply fail to realise that his concluding words are an appeal to their own selves: 'God now commands all people everywhere to repent.' Instead, they reply like polite members of a debating society: 'We will hear you again about this' (Acts 17:16ff.). In precisely the same way, Jesus looked for a response that went much deeper than intellectual adherence – much deeper than mere orthodoxy! What is involved is love, or hatred, of *his person*.

The second text is the conclusion of the Letter to the Ephesians: 'Peace be to the whole community, and love with faith, from God the Father and the Lord Jesus Christ. Grace be with all who have an undying love for our Lord Jesus Christ' (6:24). These words are quite simply a definition of what it is to be a Christian: namely, one who has received love from Jesus and who returns this love.

* * *

But what kind of 'love' is involved here? Many kinds of emotions and relationships have been given this name, then and now. If we see how Jesus filled in the contents of this word while he was on earth, we can see what his love demands of us in his encounter with us in eucharistic adoration today.

The most important text is Mt 10:37, towards the end of the discourse Jesus holds when he sends the Twelve out to preach and to heal the sick: 'Whoever loves father or mother *more than me* is not worthy of me; and whoever loves son or daughter *more than me* is not worthy of me.' We find an even stronger version of the same saying at Luke 14:26: 'Whoever comes to me and does not *hate* father and mother, wife and children, brothers and sisters, yes, and even life itself, cannot be my disciple.'

Before we rush to find some means of explaining these words away, let us hear how they are made concrete in a little story: 'To another he said, "Follow me." But he said, "Lord, first let me go and bury my father." But Jesus said to him, "Let the dead bury their own dead; but as for you, go and proclaim the kingdom of God." Another said, "I will follow you, Lord; but let me first say farewell to those at my home." Jesus said to him, "No one who puts a hand to the plough and looks back is fit for the kingdom of God"' (Lk 9:59ff.).

Surely these words are monstrous, if we take them literally? Is there any Christian alive today who could seriously claim that one who obeyed the sentiments of these words was a genuine follower of Jesus? I emphasise the word 'today' in that last sentence, because there certainly have been saints who did indeed abandon the closest members of their families to obey what they saw as a call to follow Jesus, such as St Nicholas of Flüe (d.1487), the patron saint of Switzerland, who left his wife and ten children to become a hermit, or St Jane Frances de Chantal (d.1641), who founded the Order of the Visitation after she was widowed: when her son lay down on the threshold of the house in a last attempt to prevent her from leaving, she simply stepped over him and went her way. We need not judge such saints, but we certainly cannot take them as models today! Were anyone to do so, we would surely quote against such a person other words of Jesus against those Pharisees who absolve themselves from their obligations to father and mother by pretending that their money is a sacred temple offering (Mk 7:9ff.). And what about the positive experience of married Christians who do not find themselves called to 'choose' between Jesus and the members of their families, as Matthew 10:37 suggests? What about all the positive words we hear about the Christian family from the Pope and the bishops?

All this makes it exceedingly difficult to take this saying of the Lord seriously. But it becomes even more problematic if we recall how these words must have sounded when they were first spoken in Galilee.

The duty to bury the dead was absolutely sacred in Judaism. The whole narrative of the Book of Tobit, for example, is set in motion by his steadfastness in carrying out this obligation in his exile, even though this is forbidden by the king and his neighbours laugh at him: 'If I saw the body of any of my people thrown out behind the wall of Nineveh, I would bury it. I also buried any whom King Sennacherib put to death when he came fleeing from Judaea ...' (1:17f.). How much more sacred was the obligation to bury one's own parents! Detailed regulations in Leviticus 21 and Ezekiel 44 are concerned to ensure the absolute ritual purity of the priests who exercise the cult on behalf of the people. This requires that they avoid contact with any corpse, but the precept to bury one's nearest family members was more sacred even than this obligation to remain 'undefiled': 'They shall not defile themselves by going near to a dead person; for father or mother, however, and for son or daughter, and for brother or unmarried sister they may defile themselves' (Ezk 44:25). Thus Jesus' words are not only repugnant to natural human affection. They also go directly against the law of God, and a Jew who heard them must surely have rejected them as profoundly irreligious.

There is a classic way of defusing the bombshell: we say that Jesus expected the world to end very soon, as we see for example in his words, 'Truly I tell you, there are some standing here who will not taste death until they see that the kingdom of God has come with power' (Mk 9:1). His whole horizon was dominated by this imminent expectation, we are told, and this explains the apparently impossible commands in the Sermon on the Mount ('Be perfect!') and here in Luke 9. The same would apply to Paul's advice not to get married 'in view of the impending crisis' (1 Co 7:25ff.). The disciples are entering an 'interim' existence where all the normal rules of conduct must be suspended. What is the point of burying my father, if the kingdom of God is going to break in at any moment?

This interpretation may be correct, if we ask the historical question: given that Jesus did in fact speak these words, what could he have meant by them? But this does not automatically license us to neutralise their provocation by saying that since the world did not in fact come to an end as Jesus (and Paul) expected, these terrible words have merely historical interest. For that would make them a record of what Jesus said – not of what he says today to the Church in general, and certainly not of *what he says to me personally when I kneel before him in adoration!* This is tremendously tempting, when we are faced with the appalling demands these stories make. But is there another way to react to them that does not neuter the scriptures?

The key is given in a narrative I have already quoted, the anointing of Jesus' head at Bethany. Jesus' defence of the woman who has 'performed a good service for me' includes the staggering words: 'For you always have the poor with you, and you can show kindness to them whenever you wish; but you will not always have me' (Mk 14:7). These words are an open contradiction of the precept at Deuteronomy 15:11: 'Since there will never cease to be some in need on the earth, I therefore command you, "Open your hand to the poor and needy neighbour in your land".' They are also hard to reconcile with Jesus' own identification of himself with 'the least' of those who suffer (in the parable of the sheep and goats, Mt 25:31ff.), to say nothing of the entire Christian tradition of caring for the poor and of commitment to the alleviation of suffering, which has taken so many forms and today is often invoked as a 'preferential option' of Christian activity – precisely in the spirit of Jesus! 'You will not always have me.' We may accept the challenge of these words, or we may refuse it; but there is no getting round the fact that the central reality here, dominating and deciding every other factor, is *the person of Jesus*. He demands a personal relationship of love that becomes the unconditional priority in the lives of those who follow him. This priority can be formulated, as we have seen in these texts, in a manner that normal human sentiment and the religious sensitivity of the tradition of Israel were bound to find highly offensive. Jesus put his own person so much in the centre, as the exclusive source of religious authority ('You have heard that it was said to those of ancient times ... *but I say to you ...*', Mt 5:21ff.) and the object of an unqualified adherence, that there were only two options: either to love him or to hate him.

For us who believe, the religious challenge of the person of Jesus is just as acute now as it was in Galilee and Jerusalem nineteen hundred and seventy years ago. It is to us that he addresses the terrifying invitation: 'Those who lose their life *for my sake* will find it' (Mt 10:39). The encounter with him in eucharistic adoration finds us defenceless, for there are (so to speak) no trees behind which we could seek shelter like Adam and Eve in the garden – no music or words to listen to, no theological reflections to water down the demands he makes of us, no smoke-screen of good works to hide us from his gaze. He demands everything of us, and even if we are convinced, on the level of faith, that it is his love that makes this demand, still our feelings rebel, as Francis Thompson put it in 'The Hound of Heaven' (1890):

Ah! Is Thy love indeed
A weed, albeit an amaranthine weed,
Suffering no flowers except its own to mount?
Ah! Must –
Designer infinite! –
Ah! Must Thou char the wood ere Thou canst limn with it? [...]
Whether man's heart or life it be which yields
Thee harvest, must Thy harvest-fields
Be dunged with rotten death?

It is indeed a terrible risk to say yes to God. A warning is
signposted by a saying of Jesus which has been transmitted outside
the Bible, but is judged by many scholars to be probably
authentic. It is found, for example, in the Coptic Gospel of
Thomas (nr. 82): 'The one who is near me is near the fire, but
the one who is far from me is far from the kingdom.' According
to this saying, two options – and only two options – are possible
to the one who is confronted by the radicality of Jesus Christ, and
both involve risk. I must therefore decide which risk is the more
frightening, since one of them is going to happen – there is no
third choice! Will I draw near to Jesus and risk being consumed
in the fire ('Ah! Must Thou char the wood ...?'), or will I stay at
a safe distance from him and thereby remain far from the
kingdom – an image that we could translate into modern
language as the risk of leading an inauthentic life, of failing to
become the one God wanted me to be?

Let us suppose that we take the risk of saying yes to him, the
risk of loving him. What happens then?

We discover something remarkable: the terrifying sayings of
Jesus, which were included in the yes we said to him, are not in
fact meant to be taken literally. But this does not in the least
allow us to disregard them, for they are a boundary, a threshold
that must be crossed if we are genuinely to enter the sphere where
God reigns. This is because Jesus Christ really does demand
everything of his disciples, as we see in the case of Peter.

When he says to Jesus, 'We have left everything and followed
you' (Mk 10:28), he is speaking the literal truth. Jesus shows his
concern for Peter's family by healing his mother-in-law of a high

fever, but *in the same breath* he uproots Peter completely from
this family. He must leave his wife behind while he follows Jesus.
This is a terrifyingly radical demand to make of a man in a
society with no structures that could provide a network of social
services or financial support for his wife (and children) while he
is away. Many migrant workers in our world send money home
to help their families, but Peter did not earn anything while
following the Lord, so he was not able to contribute to his own
family. It is not difficult to imagine what Peter's family and
neighbours, and other fishermen in Bethsaida, thought about the
step Peter had taken. They must have condemned him as not
only crazy, but downright immoral, when he apparently
abandoned his responsibilities to run after the rabbi from
Nazareth who had promised to make him a different kind of
'fisher'.

But Peter was not the only one to be uprooted in this way.
When Jesus replies, he indicates that many others have done the
same, by speaking in general terms of 'anyone' who has 'left
house or brothers or sisters or mother or father or children or
fields, *for my sake* and for the sake of the good news' (Mk 10:29),
and we should let ourselves taste that word 'left' – 'abandoned',
'forsaken' – in all its unlovely harshness before deciding if the
person of Jesus is really worth such a price. To say yes to him is
exceedingly costly. He is not talking about some superficial
choice that would not affect us in the depths of our being, nor
about dipping our toes into the waters of discipleship to test their
temperature (always with the possibility of withdrawing them if
those waters are too hot), but about staking literally everything
on his person. The merchant who finds a pearl of great value has
to sell absolutely everything he owns in order to buy it (Mt
12:45f.).

But Jesus adds a promise: those who have left everything will
'receive a hundredfold *now in this age* – houses, brothers and
sisters, mothers and children, and fields, with persecutions – and
in the age to come eternal life' (Mk 10:30). So we are allowed to
bury our father after all? Certainly. But only after we have taken
the words of Jesus seriously and let them shatter what we take for
granted as 'normal' existence, including our religious ideas about

what God wants; or, formulating the same encounter with him more profoundly and therefore more positively, only after we have truly made his love the pivot of our lives. And we see this too in the story of Peter. He 'abandoned' his wife to follow Jesus, but he received her back again after the resurrection, and she accompanied him on his missionary journeys, as Paul tells us (1 Co 9:5). Thus the words of the Lord at the close of 'The Hound of Heaven' need not be understood exclusively in the sense of a compensation after this life, in heaven, for the things renounced or lost here on earth by the one who says yes to 'this tremendous Lover':

> All which I took from thee I did but take,
> Not for thy harms,
> But just that thou might'st seek it in My arms.
> All which thy child's mistake
> Fancies as lost, I have stored for thee at home.
> Rise, clasp My hand, and come!

To sum up, there is nothing cosy about the relationship involved here. It is a love that lays claim to the totality of our existence in order to transform it by configuring it to Christ. The transfiguring joy is given only to those who are willing to risk the 'fire'. And this yes we say to his love must be repeated and deepened throughout our lives, for such a love requires concrete expression and genuine nourishment. Both of these can be found in the practice of silent eucharistic adoration.

6

AN ESCAPIST PRAYER?

Eucharistic adoration, as a prayer of personal love
for Jesus, has often been seen as a 'flight from the world'.
But all true Christian spirituality,
following the logic of the incarnation,
must direct us into the world, not out of it.
Adoration does this by configuring us to Christ,
so that his compassionate love lives in us.

'I am not asking you to take them out of the world,' says Jesus in his high-priestly prayer (Jn 17:15). It follows that if silent eucharistic adoration were to possess an inherent tendency to take Christians 'out of the world', that is, to distract us from the urgent commitment to help those who suffer and to challenge the unjust structures that dehumanise our fellow human beings, or if it supplied the afflicted with a consolation that was a mere analgesic to let them forget their pain for a brief space, then it could not be a prayer in keeping with the mind of Christ. It would be at best a cosy irrelevance, at worst the kind of spirituality that God rejects as perverted: 'Trample my courts no more; bringing offerings is futile; incense is an abomination to me ... When you stretch out your hands, I will hide my eyes from you; even though you make many prayers, I will not listen' (Is 1:12ff.); 'Oh, that someone among you would shut the doors, so that you would not kindle fire on my altar in vain! I have no pleasure in you, says the Lord of hosts, and I will not accept an offering from your hands' (Mal 1:10).

This objection – that silent eucharistic adoration is an escapist prayer – does not have the same apparent plausibility in the case of all forms of eucharistic devotion, for this has in fact often been directed 'out into the world' in the form of eucharistic processions, as an act of blessing the fields on rogation days, or as a public profession of faith in the presence of Jesus in the Blessed

Sacrament. I remember from my student days a procession through the streets of Göttingen in northern Germany on the feast of Corpus Christi in 1975, at the end of which the parish priest said, not without a happy pride, 'Now we have demonstrated our faith in the eyes of people who do not share it.' He had grown up under the Nazi ideology, which hated genuine faith in Jesus Christ. It was a provocative sign in the 1930s to show in public that one owed allegiance to Jesus, an action that exposed Catholics to a very real danger.

There is certainly a value in this kind of witness. People may react with hostility, or even worse with a bored indifference – like the Italians who sat smoking on their verandas while we carried the monstrance through the streets of their town – but at least they have seen what we believe in. Blessed Niels Stensen (d.1686), the Danish natural scientist, was so overwhelmed by the Corpus Christi procession in Florence in 1666 that he accepted the truth of the Catholic faith on the spot. The same thing happened to another Scandinavian, the twenty-two-year-old Kjell Arild Pollestad, in Rome in 1971:

> I have never understood what happened in St Mary Major's during that Holy Thursday Mass in commemoration of Christ's institution of the eucharist. As far as I can see, there is no trait in my character, no episode in my life that could have prepared me for such an experience or have given any kind of advance notice of it. [...] I had not even intended to go to the service; as far as I was concerned, the papal Mass on Palm Sunday had been more than enough. And now I had been filled all at once with an unshakeable conviction that what was happening here, what these people believed and professed, was the truth. I had become a believer. The door had been opened for me before I even managed to knock on it. [...] After the Mass, what remained of the consecrated Bread was borne in procession to the sacrament-chapel. [...] People began to throng even more tightly in the aisle. The procession drew nearer. Now all knelt down as the cardinal passed by them with the sacrament. Before I knew what was happening, I too was on my knees, and if ever I have seen a blessing become visible, then it was here, when the Lord's Body was borne directly in front of my eyes in the old

cardinal's hands. I still heard the echo of his sermon: *'The Lord said: This is my Body'*. With all my heart I could now have joined in those words from Thomas Aquinas' hymn:

I do not see your wounds, as Thomas did,
yet still I profess you to be my God.

No, I did not doubt
(from Father Pollestad's autobiography
Veien til Rom, Oslo, 1990).

We could perhaps say that eucharistic devotion functions here primarily as an act of witness, not only *vis-à-vis* outsiders, but also for those who join in the act of public worship and so have their faith reinforced.

But the silent adoration we are speaking of in this book is aimed not at other people, but at Jesus Christ. It does not at first sight appear to be directed to the world at all, since it is primarily an expression of love for him, and as such has its own logic. Since this love provides the *raison d'être* of eucharistic adoration, it is necessary to define it more precisely. The previous chapter looked at the quality of 'love' between the Lord and his disciples in the Gospels and said that this is precisely what is offered to us when we adore Christ in the sacrament of the altar. This chapter must tackle an objection to placing so much emphasis on love, namely, that it makes adoration an escapist form of prayer and that this is inappropriate for Christians, since it withdraws them from their task of being the salt of the earth and the light of the world.

* * *

It is, unfortunately, undeniable that Christians have frequently spoken of love for Jesus, and given this love artistic expression, in a weak and sentimental way. This makes what I have written misleading, for speaking of love could all too easily suggest a cosy picture of our relationship to Jesus as a source of consolation for people who cannot face up to the tough realities of life, or who have lost out in life's battle.

There is nothing wrong in seeking consolation. It is one of our basic religious needs, and Jesus recognises the legitimacy of this need when he says: 'Come to me, all you that are weary and are carrying heavy burdens, and I will give you rest' (Mt 11:28). He does not tell us to repress our anxieties and fears, but to bring them to him. It is quite simply impossible for a normal human being to go through life without being wounded in one way or another, and very often this means deep wounds in human hearts. Thus the sentiments expressed by Francis Stanfield (d.1914) in his hymn 'Sweet Sacrament Divine' may certainly have a place in our relationship with Christ in the eucharist:

> Sweet sacrament of peace,
> dear home of every heart,
> where restless yearnings cease,
> and sorrows all depart:
> there in thine ear all trustfully
> we tell our tale of misery,
> sweet sacrament of peace.
>
> Sweet sacrament of rest,
> Ark from the ocean's roar,
> within thy shelter blest
> soon may we reach the shore;
> save us, for still the tempest raves;
> save, lest we sink beneath the waves,
> sweet sacrament of rest.

These words, which are acceptable as the expression of one element in our relationship to the Lord, do however become very problematic indeed, if they are allowed to define the entirety of that relationship. For then we are tempted to try to escape from created reality, which we experience as something negative. An endless procession of Christian preachers and writers down through the centuries have proclaimed the necessity of flight from the world, and eucharistic adoration, because of its character as an intimate expression of love for the Lord, can too easily be seen as the instrument of such a flight. Stanfield's hymn with its unforgettable melody, so popular among many generations of Catholics, certainly tends in this direction. After speaking of yearnings, sorrows, misery, the ocean's roar, the tempest and the waves, it ends thus:

> Sweet light, so shine on us, we pray,
> that earthly joys may fade away,
> sweet sacrament divine.

The message is clear: 'earthly joys' are illusory, and the only genuine joy is to be found by taking refuge in the Jesus who awaits us (as Stanfield says in the first verse) 'hid in thy earthly throne', the tabernacle. Another hymn from my Scottish childhood underlines the same point:

> I rise from dreams of time,
> and an angel guides my feet
> to the sacred altar-throne
> where Jesus' heart doth beat ...

The dimension of time, which so profoundly structures our entire existence, is here unmasked (so to speak) as nothing more than insubstantial 'dreams', out of which we must be led to the truth of the tabernacle.

We find Stanfield's message, that the tabernacle is a source of consolation, in John Betjeman's poem 'Felixstowe, or The Last of Her Order' (1958). The second and third strophes run as follows:

> In winter when the sea winds chill and shriller
> Than those of summer, all their cold unload
> Full on the gimcrack attic of the villa
> Where I am lodging off the Orwell Road,
> I put my final shilling in the meter
> And only make my loneliness completer.
>
> In eighteen ninety-four when we were founded,
> Counting our Reverend Mother we were six,
> How full of hope we were and prayer-surrounded,

'The Little Sisters of the Hanging Pyx'.
We built our orphanage. We ran our school.
Now only I am left to keep the rule.

The last two strophes run:

Across the grass the poplar shades grow longer
And louder clang the waves along the coast.
The band packs up. The evening breeze is stronger
And all the world goes home to tea and toast.
I hurry past a cakeshop's tempting scones
Bound for the red brick twilight of St John's.

'Thou knowest my down sitting and mine uprising'
Here where the white light burns with steady glow
Safe from the vain world's silly sympathizing,
Safe with the Love that I was born to know,
Safe from the surging of the lonely sea
My heart finds rest, my heart finds rest in Thee.

This final strophe begins with a quotation from Psalm 139 and
closes with the first words of St Augustine's 'Confessions'. And it
is no accident that the old nun emphasises the wind and the sea
and the 'vain world' outside the church, and that she uses the
word 'safe' three times, as she encounters 'the Love that I was
born to know' in her prayer *before the tabernacle* (the sanctuary
lamp in many Anglican churches is white, rather than red as is
usual in Catholic churches). The marvellously sustained
ambivalence of Betjeman's poem means that it can be read
equally well as a triumphant affirmation of the lonely old nun
who finds consolation in front of the tabernacle or as a pitiless
unmasking of the frustrated emptiness of her old age, depending
on what one prefers to hear in these lines. It may even be wrong
to formulate this as an either/or question. The important point
in our context is not to ask what the poet himself meant, but
simply to *absorb* the image he paints with such clarity.

We find the same basic image, this time with no ambivalence,
in Gerard Manley Hopkins' portrayal of the contemplative

religious life as a flight from a dangerous world, in his poem 'Heaven-Haven', subtitled 'A nun takes the veil' (1864):

> I have desired to go
> Where springs not fail,
> To fields where flies no sharp and sided hail
> And a few lilies blow.
>
> And I have asked to be
> Where no storms come,
> Where the green swell is in the havens dumb,
> And out of the swing of the sea.

The images are perfectly clear – and very dangerous! This understanding of the contemplative religious life wholly consecrated to prayer as an attempt (perhaps more or less successful in individual cases) to escape from the threatening complexities of existence in the world to a supposed refuge 'where no storms come' is probably much more widespread, even among committed and informed Catholics, than the more accurate understanding of this form of the Christian life as a participation in Jesus' naked struggle against the devil in the wilderness. But it is fatal to misunderstand our relationship to Jesus in this way. He makes it very clear in his high-priestly prayer that his disciples are not to be 'of the world', just as he himself is not 'of the world'. But – as I wrote above – he also says: 'I am not asking you to take them out of the world.' Spirituality therefore means a balancing act between being 'in the world' while not 'of the world'.

And we do all live in the world, as a matter of sheer *fact*. We cannot opt out of our society in the pure form that Hopkins' poem so powerfully evokes, for God himself became a member of human society, and that is where he has placed us. For even if it is true that 'our citizenship is in heaven' (Ph 3:20) and we are 'aliens and exiles' here on earth (1 P 2:11), so that we must be detached from the values of the world ('Do not be conformed to this world' [Rm 12:2]), nevertheless God's words to the Jewish exiles in Babylon apply to us too: 'Seek the welfare of the city *where I have sent you* into exile, and pray to the Lord on its behalf, for in its welfare you will find your welfare' (Jr 29:7). Our involvement in the world in which we live is ultimately nothing other than the consequence of our belief in the incarnation: namely, our belief that God entered all the structures of created existence in order to heal them from within. A spirituality which empties the world of all positive value and preaches flight from it fails to take the incarnation seriously: all true Christian spirituality leads in some way *into the world,* not out of it. Tyrants will never be troubled by a spirituality of flight from the world. Indeed, they will encourage it, as in Latin America in the 1980s, where the CIA promoted the growth of Pentecostal Churches and dictators supported Archbishop Marcel Lefebvre's movement within the Catholic Church, since both were seen as excellent lines of defence against those 'subversive' Christians who took the *societal* implications of the Gospel seriously.

So we must face the question: is eucharistic adoration an escapist form of prayer? The texts from Stanfield and Betjeman certainly suggest that this is the case. But this is not the whole story.

*   *   *

In his obituary of the Anglican priest David Randall, published in *The Guardian* on 16 August 1996, Kenneth Leech writes: 'He was a founder member of the Jubilee Group, a network of socialist Christians. Like many politically radical Christians, he had a very traditional theology with a strong emphasis on the daily office, prayer and *eucharistic adoration*' (my italics). Randall seems to have displayed a startling eclecticism: Leech writes that St Clement's 'was probably the only church in the world to have a shrine for racial justice focused on a statue of Our Lady of Fatima, beneath which was printed the Litany of Our Lady of the Freedom Fighters'. But there is nothing artificial about the connection between Randall's esteem for eucharistic adoration and his intense commitment to the poor of London's housing estates and to Aids sufferers. On the contrary, he had grasped what eucharistic adoration is all about: immersion in the compassion of Christ, which we then must bring to the world's pain; letting ourselves be set ablaze by his light, which we then must bring to the world's darkness.

In precisely the same way, the Missionaries of Charity have learned from Mother Teresa that their contemplation of Jesus in the eucharist in their chapel leads directly to their encounter with him in the poorest of the poor on the streets. Without the contemplation of the Christ who is hidden under the veil of the sacrament, they would not be able to recognise the Christ who is hidden under the veil of the outcasts.

Adoration would indeed be an escapist form of prayer if it allowed us to remain *separate from* Jesus. For then it would not touch us in our depths. We would be in control of our relationship to the Lord, making him a gift of measured amounts of our time and our attention, loving him to a certain degree, no doubt, but not truly united to him. And of course it is always possible to misuse eucharistic adoration (like every other form of prayer) in this way, as a pious Maginot Line we erect to prevent God from encroaching on our lives and conquering them so that he can *act* in them; and it is our tragedy if this Maginot Line proves more successful than the one erected in France between the Wars.

But eucharistic adoration need not remain on this superficial level. On the contrary, it has the power to transform our lives in the most radical manner, through an osmosis that configures us to Christ and thereby sends us out into the world.

*   *   *

In Galatians 4:19 Paul speaks of 'Christ taking shape' or 'being formed'. This process begins when we 'clothe ourselves in Christ' in baptism (3:27) and will be fully accomplished only when Christ returns at the close of history to 'transform the body of our humiliation that it may be conformed to the body of his glory, by the power that also enables him to make all things subject to himself' (Ph 3:21). The Christian life can thus be seen as a continuing process of configuration to Christ.

Paul very consciously presents himself in his letters as one who is on this path, especially when he rebukes the Corinthians for having misguided ideas of what an apostle ought to be. They have been deceived by 'super-apostles' (see especially 2 Co 10-11) and do not understand that the one who leads the community must follow Christ in taking the last place, not the highest: 'I think that God has exhibited us apostles as last of all, as though sentenced to death ... we are hungry and thirsty, we are poorly clothed and beaten and homeless, and we grow weary from the work of our own hands ... we have become like the rubbish of the world, the dregs of all things, to this very day' (1 Co 4:9ff.). Only *this* experience can allow Paul to write words which otherwise would be intolerably arrogant: 'Be imitators of me, as I am of Christ' (11:1).

The first instrument of this osmosis is Jesus' word. 'You have been cleansed by the word that I have spoken to you', he tells the apostles (Jn 15:3). This word must dwell in our heart, in the very depths of our being, just as the recollection of the events concerning Jesus was preserved in Mary's heart (Lk 2:19, 51). We must contemplate this word with love and let it resonate within us.

Cardinal Cardijn's Young Christian Workers made famous the slogan 'See – Judge – Act' which has been taken up more recently as a hermeneutical tool in Latin American liberation theology and basic communities too. Applied to the Bible, this means that my reading should lead to reflection, and reflection to action: in other words, I should always be asking the question, 'What does this text mean for my life?'

This is, obviously, one vitally important key to unlock the message of scripture, since we are safe in assuming that when God speaks to us in his word, this will have practical consequences for us. But it is surely not the only way to read scripture. I may in fact be preventing God from speaking to me in the way the Holy Spirit wants here and now, precisely because I have the expectation that every text of scripture is always going to contain concrete moral guidance or specific directives for the conduct of my life or of society. Perhaps all he wants today is to show me a picture of Jesus as he moves about in Galilee and Jerusalem, or to remind me of God's fidelity to his promises as I read the Old Testament. Perhaps all he wants today is to let me listen to Jesus speaking to me, as one friend to another. Growth in friendship is a process that discloses more and more of my friend to me; so it is with Jesus too. This process is an imperceptible osmosis that configures me more and more to him. By listening to him, by seeing the way he acts, I take on his way of looking at things – and this is what Paul means when he writes, 'Let the same mind be in you that was in Christ Jesus' (Ph 2:5).

It is worth recalling here that the books of the Bible were written in cultures where silent reading was unknown, and that the custom of reading aloud on one's own lasted for many centuries. There is a letter from a medieval monk in which he laments that he is unable for the time being to read the Bible – not because of problems with his eyesight, but because he has a persistently sore throat! In our culture, if we see people reading aloud on their own, or forming the words with their lips as they read, we tend to assume that they have reading difficulties. But I have found it very valuable to read scripture aloud on my own, and I believe that this is always good, provided of course that one can do this without disturbing others. In this way, the eye sees God's word, the tongue speaks it, and the ear hears it – and thus the word enters much more deeply into my heart, and imprints itself much more profoundly on my memory. It is good to read slowly and give the word *time* to sink into myself.

Christ also gives us his sacraments as instruments of the same osmosis. Every time I participate in the Mass, I experience Christ's total self-giving. He holds nothing back for himself: on the Cross, everything that was his was given away, in an act which was at once the supreme adoration of the Father and the supreme expression of his love for us, and the eucharist makes present this same sacrifice so that we may be drawn into the same movement of self-giving. The Catholic tradition has always insisted that his presence in the sacrament is unconditional, an absolute gift, in such a way that he does not withhold the gift of his own self even where there is no answering love or faith in the one who receives communion. If I share consciously in this mystery, I *must* be drawn into the logic of Christ's boundless love for the Father and for the world. Thus I learn to lead a 'eucharistic' life, giving more and more of myself.

The same process ought to take place when I receive the forgiveness of my sins in the sacrament of penance. Here, I am drawn into the dynamic of Jesus' love for sinners, and I learn the lesson of the parable he tells, in the context of his discourse on the community life of his disciples (Mt 18), about the chain of forgiveness: 'I forgave you all that debt because you pleaded with me', says the king. 'Should not you have had mercy on your fellow slave, as I had mercy on you?' It is to me that the Lord addresses these words, and it now becomes something natural for me to pardon my fellow servant the trifling sum I am owed.

The adoration of Jesus in the eucharist has this same power to configure my life to his. It is of course true to say that I can learn much from him here, where he is utterly exposed to me and I grow in the capacity to expose myself to him. But the principal aim of adoration is most definitely not to learn something. It is an expression of love, and needs no other justification than the words of St Bernard of Clairvaux (d.1153), *amo ut amem,* 'I love in order that I may love'. Since our human love is always fragile, it must continually be strengthened in this encounter with the Lord, so that it becomes configured to his divine loving.

In particular, our love becomes configured to his unending compassion, and this is why eucharistic adoration, if undertaken with openness to the Lord and an authentic desire to become more and more like him, is no escapist prayer, but something that sends us out into the world – as messengers of hope.

Our world certainly needs hope. It is of course a cliché to say that the media overlook the good news and bombard us with the bad news. But even the very pious Norwegian newspaper which landed on my doormat one dark morning in January 1995, despite all its efforts to bring information that would edify its readers, could not avoid telling them about many terrible events. On page 11, for example, alongside a photograph of the Pope celebrating Mass in Manila with a congregation of more than four million – the largest number ever in Christian history to gather for an act of worship – there was an article about the refusal of the warring parties in Bosnia to respect a cease-fire on which they had agreed, and short pieces about an explosion in a Chinese warehouse and about conflicts in Somalia, Algeria and

Northern Ireland. The allegedly imminent divorce of Prince Charles and Princess Diana, with the potential effect on their children, was also mentioned. All this on one single page of a newspaper!

I have insisted in this chapter that eucharistic adoration is not to be understood as an escape from the turmoils of the world in which God has called us to live. How then can our act of adoration be related to what we see going on?

The answer is twofold: it can be a profession of faith in Christ's compassion, and an act of intercession.

PART THREE

THE FRUIT

7

THOSE WHO HAVE HOPE

The Christian answer to the problem of suffering
is no intellectual solution,
but the person of Christ,
who shares in human suffering from within.
His compassion tells us that
even where we cannot see any possible meaning,
suffering is not meaningless.

The two most central acts of our worship include a solemn profession of faith, namely baptism and the Sunday liturgy. But these only make explicit something present in absolutely every act of prayer, whether there are four million persons taking part or only one. Prayer is always an act that makes my faith known, either to others who see me praying or else simply to my own self: if I did not believe in God, I would not set aside time to be with him.

God created us to find our fulfilment in loving him and worshipping him here on earth, and eternally in heaven. Thus faith in God necessarily includes a hope for the future.

Neither faith nor hope can be taken for granted. Those who do in fact believe should never underestimate how difficult it is for many people today to believe in a God who is allegedly 'almighty' and 'love' and yet does nothing to stop untold millions from dying in earthquakes, in epidemics like Spanish influenza after the First World War or Aids today, or in famines caused by drought and crop failure. It is not easy to believe in an almighty and loving God who does not intervene to stop untold millions from dying in war, or as a result of the wickedness of their political leaders who cold-bloodedly employ famine as an instrument to attain their goals. To mention only one example, it has been estimated that 'between 27 and 43 millions' starved to death in China in the Great Leap Forward, and the staggering imprecision of that statistic reminds us how many of the victims of collective and state inhumanity remain forever anonymous, deprived even of the right to a tombstone. One can add endlessly to the list of difficulties for faith in God. Why, for example, does he apparently remain inactive while entire populations languish under crushing dictatorships for the whole of their lives? Why does he permit politicians in the western democracies to implement social policies that drive more and more people into poverty? Or why does he not prevent all the accidents that bring death to travellers by air, land and sea? I have been told that Fratel Gino, a priest bearing the stigmata who lives at San Vitorchiano outside Rome, once saw a plane falling from the sky and that his powerful intercession saved it from crashing. This (assuming for the sake of argument the truth of this story) would be a mighty testimony to the power of God, but it undeniably prompts the question: if he can do this with one plane, why not with all? Exactly the same harsh question is prompted by reports of miraculous healings: why are only some sick persons healed, not all?

CNN, Internet and other instruments of instant communication link up the whole world and make us visually informed. A mere fifty years ago, we might not even have heard of the world-wide streams of refugees or of ethnic conflicts such as those in Rwanda in 1994, still less seen pictures of them, but now fresh film from the most remote of war-torn countries can be seen in every home. This increased awareness can certainly make our prayer more concrete, but at the same time it intensifies the challenge to faith, since this challenge can now be presented in a visual form which picks up images immediately recognisable to all who share the common framework of the cultural references of the last fifty years of world history. Most of these cultural references are as a matter of sheer fact visual, rather than aural or verbal as they were in the first half of this century and in earlier times. This is why the visual word 'icon' is so often used of figures as diverse as Mother Teresa and Marilyn Monroe, and why political evaluations can so often be encapsulated in images (for example, Margaret Thatcher's handbag and Imelda Marcos' shoes) which need no detailed unpacking. Universally-shared images such as the tanks rolling into Prague in 1968 or the moon landing in 1969, or, more recently, the fall of the Berlin Wall or the handshakes between Jewish and Palestinian leaders on the White House lawn, have a profoundly defining significance; as the cliché puts it, all those above a certain age know where they were the day President Kennedy was shot in Dallas.

All this makes it impossible to brush aside as a mere emotional outburst questions like: 'Where was God in Auschwitz?', 'Where was God when the Khmer Rouge killed a third of the population of Cambodia?' For these are vivid visual formulations of an immensely serious theological problem.

I can ask the same question in the context of my own personal history. Why does the God who is almighty and loving do nothing to prevent millions of innocent children and adults from suffering lacerating emotional pain and terrible insecurity in their most fundamental family relationships, through sexual abuse or infidelity? The urgent theological question posed in the last paragraph can also be personalised: 'Where was God when I was raped?', 'Where was God when I lost my job?'

It would be simple if we could take the line of Job's friends in the Bible and attribute all these calamities to God's just punishment of human sins, and it is of course the case that Christians past and present have very often interpreted public and private catastrophes in keeping with the friends of Job.

But Jesus himself excludes the possibility of this answer. When he is told about 'the Galileans whose blood Pilate had mingled with their sacrifices' (i.e. those who are killed by the political power), he denies the potential implication that 'they were worse sinners than all the other Galileans'. Likewise, he denies that 'those eighteen who were killed when the tower of Siloam fell on them' (i.e. those who die in an accident) 'were worse offenders than all the others living in Jerusalem' (Lk 13:1ff.). The Fourth Gospel completes this message by extending it to include illness. When the disciples see the man born blind and ask their logically absurd – but very human! – question, 'Rabbi, who sinned, this man or his parents, that he was born blind?', Jesus rejects the causal link they posit between suffering and sin: 'Neither this man nor his parents sinned' (Jn 9:2f.). And so, whenever this link is posited by Christians today, openly or implicitly, we must object vigorously: What did the unborn child do to 'deserve' being born dependent on narcotics? Can we really assert that those liquidated by Stalin or Mao all 'deserved' to be sent to labour camps or shot? No, reality under the governance of God is more complicated than Job's friends thought.

The Old Testament too knows perfectly well that prosperity often falls to the lot of the wicked: 'for they have no pain; their bodies are sound and sleek. They are not in trouble as others are; they are not plagued like other people' (Ps 73:3f.). It is scarcely surprising that the psalmist's first reaction is cynical: 'All in vain have I kept my heart clean and washed my hands in innocence. For all day long I have been plagued, and am punished every morning.' From this position, there is only a short path to the conclusion that faith in a loving and almighty God is meaningless; and we see this conclusion being drawn when an angel cries out to Gideon, 'The Lord is with you, you mighty warrior!', but only elicits the sour and bitter reply, 'But sir, if the Lord is with us, why then has all this happened to us? And where are all his wonderful deeds that our ancestors recounted to us?' (Jg 6:12f.).

Both Psalm 73 and Judges 6, when read as a whole, show God intervening to bring the troubled believer to the conviction that he does in fact exist and that faith in his loving power is supremely meaningful. But for very many of our contemporaries this faith has evaporated. Most people in western Europe still believe in the existence of a higher power, but not of a Father who is actively involved in the world. What is our response to this?

* * *

Paul tells the Thessalonians that they are not to 'grieve as others do who have no hope. For since we believe that Jesus died and rose again, even so, through Jesus, God will bring with him those who have died' (1 Th 4:13f.). This reminds us that the Christian hope is not based on reasonings that (like the 'natural moral law') are in principle accessible to anyone who takes the trouble to think seriously about the realities of human life. The Christian faith does not supply any intellectually satisfactory solution to the question of what suffering might mean. Our 'answer' is the person of Jesus Christ. Our hope is based directly on our conviction that he has passed through death to the absolute life of the resurrection and that therefore death, and all the forces of destruction which we experience, do not have the final word. He has broken their power.

It is the person of Jesus that gives us hope for our own selves. 'If Christ has not been raised, your faith is futile', writes Paul (1 Co 15:17). His incarnation has united him to us indissolubly, and so his destiny has consequences for ours. As the Preface of the Mass on the feast of the Ascension says, 'Christ is the beginning, the head of the Church; where he has gone, we hope to follow.'

The Christian life always involves an essentially hidden dimension, since 'we walk by faith, not by sight' (2 Co 5:7). Thus it will always be possible for others to dismiss it as a wish-fulfilment, an illusion; and since we ourselves do not see God face-to-face, or hear a voice speaking to us directly from heaven, it will likewise always be possible for us to doubt the reality of what we believe. This is why our faith must be continually strengthened through the encounter with the living person of Jesus, so that it can stand up to the immense challenges to which it is exposed in our culture. And here I wish to draw on my own experience of the silent prayer of eucharistic adoration, to suggest that it gives our faith the nourishment we need, if we are to confront the reality and the problem of suffering. In particular, eucharistic adoration allows us to experience *Christ's compassion with his brothers and sisters.* He tells us, in the experience of this compassion, that *suffering is not meaningless* and that *he is with us in our suffering.*

Everything in this chapter is the direct fruit of the adoration of Jesus in the Blessed Sacrament. It attempts to put into theological words an experience that I hope readers too may come to share, if they open themselves to this form of prayer.

* * *

We sometimes hear that the Passion was the inevitable result of the conflict between Jesus and the religious leaders of his day (the moral being that we must take his unflinching fidelity to his proclamation of the Father's love as the model for our own conduct).

We need not deny that this is true and important. The problem, however, is that it leaves the Passion on the level of *human* action and interaction, where it almost becomes a kind of by-product. If the essential thing is Jesus' exemplary fidelity, it becomes difficult to see what positive message the Passion itself could really have for us.

On this human level, the Gospels show that Jesus could have avoided suffering, had he so wished. He does sometimes make tactical withdrawals, for example from the menacing crowd who want to throw him down from the cliff on which Nazareth is built (Lk 4:29f.), or from those who want to stone him in the temple: 'Jesus hid himself' (Jn 8:59); 'Jesus no longer walked about openly among the Jews' (11:54). But these evasive actions are never a definitive flight. He has no intention of going to the Dispersion among the Greeks outside Palestine (Jn 7:35), and when some friendly Pharisees urge him: 'Get away from here, for Herod wants to kill you', his reply indicates that he is well aware that his ministry will end in his death: 'Today, tomorrow and the next day I must be on my way, because it is impossible for a prophet to be killed outside of Jerusalem' (Lk 13:31ff.).

The predictions of his Passion show, however, that more than a mere human inevitability is involved here, more than the closing in of the net upon the courageous preacher, such as happened in Nazi Germany with priests like Blessed Rupert Mayer (d.1945). For after Peter's confession that he is the Messiah, Jesus 'began to teach them that the Son of Man must undergo great suffering ... he said all this quite openly.' Peter cannot reconcile this with his own understanding of what a Messiah ought to be, and so Jesus must rebuke him sharply: 'Get behind me, Satan! For you are setting your mind not on divine things but on human things' (Mk 8:27ff.).

Thus the passion is not to be explained in solely human terms. Its divine necessity belongs to the essence of Jesus' ministry: 'The Son of Man *must* undergo great suffering', 'Was it not *necessary* that the Messiah should suffer these things?' (Lk 24:26). Abraham's son Isaac was spared by God; but the Father 'did not withhold his own Son, but gave him up for all of us' (Rm 8:32).

If we then ask *why* the divine plan meant that Jesus had to die on the Cross for our salvation, we can find various attempts at an answer in the course of Church history, perhaps most influentially in the theology of St Anselm of Canterbury (d.1109) which speaks of the necessity to satisfy divine justice: only God made man could offer the infinite sacrifice which would be commensurate with the enormity of human sin, and indeed would outweigh this. We need not examine the theologies of the Cross here, for the point I wish to emphasise is very simple and is not dependent on any one interpretation of the Passion: if it is true that Jesus' death means life for us, as the New Testament and the entire Christian tradition unanimously teach, then – irrespective of the extent to which we can grasp the meaning of this death with our understanding – *suffering cannot be simply meaningless.*

Sometimes we can understand the potentially positive meaning of suffering, for example when we look back on a period of mental or physical sickness or other misfortune, and find that this experience has enriched and deepened us. Or we find that we can make our own the words of Virgil's Dido:

> Since I am not ignorant of ills,
> I learn how to come to the aid of those in distress

(*Aeneid* II,630). But, in practice, it will most often be difficult, or simply impossible, to understand how a specific experience of suffering can be meaningful. For many human situations are genuinely tragic.

It often seems very hard for Christians to accept the reality of human tragedy. Their belief that Jesus has 'abolished death and brought life and immortality to light' (2 Tm 1:10) seems to handicap them when they are confronted by meaninglessness, and this can result in two false moves.

We see the first in Job's friends, who devalue the seriousness of present suffering by all too hastily promising a 'happy ending': 'Do you not know ... that the exulting of the wicked is short, and the joy of the godless is but for a moment?' asks Zophar the

Naamathite. 'Even though they mount up high as the heavens,
and their head reaches to the clouds, they will perish forever like
their own dung; those who have seen them will say, "Where are
they?"' (20:4ff.). Job protests at great length that this is utterly
unrealistic: 'How often is the lamp of the wicked put out? How
often does calamity come upon them? How often does God
distribute pains in his anger? ...' (21:17); but perhaps the best
commentary on the facile assurances of Job's friends – and of so
many Christians who have taken the same line – is Miss Prism's
brief description (in Wilde's *The Importance of Being Earnest*) of
the novel she had written: 'The good ended happily, and the bad
unhappily. That is what Fiction means.'

The second false move is the rush to import a 'meaning' that
can be conferred on other people's suffering. But this is seldom
truly helpful. The Norwegian detective novelist Anne Holt has an
acidly acute parody of this Christian reaction in one of her books,
when Inspector Hanne Wilhelmsen attends the funeral of the
woman whose murder she is investigating, and notes during the
sermon how 'The lady from the Salvation Army who sat beside
her sobbed and nodded at every word and was clearly in
agreement with the parson that it was God's intention that the
little red-haired girl who was now running up and down the aisle
should grow up without a mother' (*Demonens död*, 1995).

Indeed, what meaning am I supposed to find in the death by
heart attack of a sixteen-year-old girl? Or what meaning am I
supposed to find in the hopeless cycle of poverty and dependence
from which so many people in our modern industrialised
societies will, as a matter of fact, never escape? If we are honest,
we are left with terrible questions: 'Why this?', 'Why me?' The
answer which the crucified Christ gives to such questioning is
seldom addressed to our intellects. He appeals today, as when he
lived on earth, to our faith – as the commitment our personal
love makes *to his person*. If God made man freely took suffering
upon himself, then I can believe and hope that all the devastation
I see around me and in my own life is not merely waste. There is
a meaning to it, even if it is not a meaning I shall come to know
here on earth.

It is important here to note that the Resurrection does not

wipe out the fact that Jesus has suffered. He still bears the marks of his Passion in his hands and feet and side, not only as a proof of his identity ('Look at my hands and my feet; see that it is I myself', Lk 24:39), but also to teach us that his experience of having suffered is something he bears with him into heaven. Throughout all eternity, he is 'the Lamb that was slain' (Rv 5:6; 13:8), in sharpest contradistinction to the Antichrist, whose 'mortal wound has been healed' – a sure sign that he is an impostor (13:3,12). For Jesus' wounds are indeed transfigured and glorified, so that 'Christ, being raised from the dead, will never die again' (Rm 6:9); but his invitation to Thomas, 'Reach out your hand and *put it in my side*' (Jn 20:27), shows that they have not been healed as ordinary human wounds heal, finally leaving no trace on the body – these wounds remain open.

This too has a message for us. In a posthumously published meditation on the Apostles' Creed, Hans Urs von Balthasar (d.1988) speaks of suffering as excavating 'craters' in us that will be filled with heavenly joy. The point is that these craters are not mere blemishes to be levelled out by the Resurrection, like the holes in a road surface hastily filled in before a visiting dignitary comes to open the new council chambers. For the experience of suffering is not something superficial that can be erased as lightly as the touch of a key erases the words written on a computer screen, leaving everything as it was before. It is one of the factors that make me the person I am. When I appear in heaven before God, I do not discard this experience as something henceforth irrelevant to my eternal identity: the fact of having experienced suffering in some specific way gives me a correspondingly specific receptivity to the overflowing fullness of life and joy in God's presence.

* * *

It is important not to make claims that are too precise, when we speak about the relationship between future bliss in heaven and present suffering on earth. I have in mind here the idea of a future compensation that will make good present suffering. This notion is undeniably found in the Bible: 'Blessed are you who are hungry now, for you will be filled. Blessed are you who weep now, for you will laugh' (Lk 6:21). We may leave aside here the question of whether these beatitudes refer (as Jesus or the evangelist understood them) to a reversal of fortunes already here on earth or only after death, in heaven; for another text of scripture makes it clear that when there is no realistic prospect of such a redress here on earth, this hope can go so far as to envisage a literal restoration in heaven of the losses inflicted by earthly suffering. We read in 2 Maccabees, in the story of the mother and seven brothers tortured and killed by King Antiochus for their fidelity to the Jewish law: 'The third was the victim of their sport. When it was demanded, he quickly put out his tongue and courageously stretched forth his hands, and said nobly, "I got these from Heaven [a reverential way of saying: from God], and because of his laws I disdain them, and from him I hope to get them back again"' (7:10f.).

This language of a wholly literal restitution is, however, very problematical if we forget that it is an *image,* the vivid visual expression of an utterly confident hope in God, and treat it as if it were a piece of factual information (so to speak) about eternal life. For what it would amount to, if taken literally, is nothing less than the reversal of history:

> Christ the uncrucified,
> Christ the discrucified, his death undone,
> His agony unmade, his cross dismantled

– as Edwin Muir (d.1959) puts it in his poem 'Transfiguration'. But such an undoing of history, alluring though it may be when one considers the appalling things human beings have done to one another, would mean nothing less than the dismantling of my own personal identity. I am the person who has experienced suffering (and joy) in particular ways; take away the experience, and I necessarily become a different person! This means that when I come to God, the fact of my earthly suffering is not going to be 'unmade'. For Christ cannot be discrucified: on the contrary, as I wrote above, his wounds remain open.

What then does this mean? It means – to take another biblical example – that the holy innocents, the small children killed by Herod in his attempt to take the life of the infant Jesus (Mt 2:16ff.), remain small children in heaven. They do not get the chance to grow up and live a normal human life. The poet Prudentius (d.405) captures this in a wonderfully moving image:

> *aram ante ipsam simplices*
> *palma et coronis luditis*

> before the very altar of heaven,
> with all the simplicity of children, you are playing
> with your palm-branches and crowns.

But the holy innocents are not disadvantaged by the fact that they were taken off (as Prudentius says) 'on the very threshold of the light of day ... like roses that were just budding'. In some way that is literally unimaginable for us while we live in the conditions of earthly existence, their terribly truncated lives open them to receive an unending joy in heaven that somehow makes sense of the tragedy of their slaughter. The same is true of the terrible suffering of their mothers and fathers. Matthew applies to them the words of Jeremiah, 'Rachel weeping for her children; she refused to be consoled, because they are no more'(31:15). In some way we cannot imagine, still less understand here on earth, Rachel will be consoled in heaven.

Let me stress the word 'unimaginable'. We do not *know* how the slaughter of babies can be meaningful, and we must guard against implying the grotesque image of God as a divine sadist whose will involves having babies killed. This is a question of *faith,* based on the person of the Jesus who accepted death on a cross because he loved us. Only faith – no human logic – can accept the truth of his words to Julian of Norwich, 'All shall be well, and all shall be well, and all manner of thing shall be well.'

Faith is usually naked, but sometimes the Lord lifts a little corner of the veil. This happened for me one day in summer 1991, and it happened *in the course of eucharistic adoration.* I had promised to preach at the silver jubilee Mass of my Carmelite cousin in Scotland, so I had to leave Norway for a weekend, just as a close friend of mine was dying. The first thing Brother Gunther said to me when I came back was: 'Thomas died on Saturday.' I went into our little house-chapel with its disproportionately large altar and there, very close to the host, I prayed for Thomas. He was such a good person that it seemed unnatural to ask the Lord to forgive him his sins, as one normally does for the dead. Thomas had no patience whatever with sham, so it seemed improper to use standard, ritualised words that did not really fit him. So I found myself praying: 'Lord, bring him into your joy!' And all of a sudden I experienced something I can only describe as waves of joy flowing through the dark little basement chapel and transforming it into a place of extraordinary light. This seemed to me then – and still seems to me – a little hint from the Lord that all the terrible suffering of this man who died so young, at the age of twenty-five, was taken up into the illimitable compassion of the God in whom he had believed, and that, in some way utterly beyond human comprehension, all was 'made well' for Thomas.

*   *   *

The figure of Christ on the Cross assures us that suffering is not mere meaninglessness, because *he shares in our suffering.* The risen Jesus cannot suffer in his own person, for 'death no longer has dominion over him' (Rm 6:9), yet when he speaks to Saul outside Damascus, he does not say: 'Saul, Saul, why do you persecute those who believe in me?', but: 'Saul, Saul, *why do you persecute me? ... I am Jesus, whom you are persecuting*' (Acts 9:4f.). His parable of the sheep and the goats (Mt 25) goes even further than this, by showing that his compassion is not limited only to a share in the sufferings of those who are explicitly his disciples. He is present in every human being who suffers: 'I was hungry ... I was thirsty ... I was a stranger ... I was naked ... I was sick ... I was in prison.'

The idea of an all-embracing divine mercy is found already in the Old Testament, where the Book of Jonah portrays the clash between the prophet's narrow concern and the universal concern of the Lord, which extends beyond the boundaries of his chosen people to include the pagan mariners, who 'feared the Lord, and offered a sacrifice to the Lord and made vows' (1:16), and the pagan city of Nineveh, 'in which there are more than a hundred and twenty thousand persons who do not know their right hand from their left' (4:11). A sentence of Sirach sums this up: 'The mercy (*eleos*) of a human being is for one's neighbour, but the mercy (*eleos*) of the Lord is for all flesh' (18:13 in a literal translation). Less literal renderings of this verse translate the Greek word as 'compassion'; but the idea of a genuine divine compassion, of God's sharing intimately in human suffering from within, is not in fact present in this text. This idea has to wait until Jesus comes.

The word 'compassion' is often used in a weak sense, to indicate a reaction from the outside to other people's suffering, a mentality that condescends from on high, dividing the human race into benefactors and recipients (for example, in the case of aid to underdeveloped countries); so it is not surprising that the whole concept of compassion should be rejected by so many today in favour of other concepts like justice and rights. But I think it is still possible to salvage the word, if we pay heed to its etymology. The Latin root of 'compassion' (like the Greek root of 'sympathy') means something much more radical, namely a direct share in someone else's suffering. The word is used in this way at Hebrews 10:32ff.: 'Recall those earlier days when, after you had been enlightened, you endured a hard struggle with sufferings [of your own, *pathêmatôn*], sometimes being publicly exposed to abuse and persecution, and sometimes being partners with those so treated. For you had compassion for [*sunepathêsate*, literally: you shared in suffering with] those who were in prison.' The same verb is used of Jesus at Hebrews 4:15: 'We do not have a high priest who is unable to sympathise with [*sumpathêsai*, literally: to share in suffering] our weaknesses.' He is not aloof on a throne of transcendent majesty – he is the freezing beggar whom Martin of Tours clothes with his soldier's cloak. He stands beside us and shares our suffering *from within*.

Nor should we limit our vision of his compassion, as if he shared only in the sufferings of the persecuted righteous, or of those the Victorians called 'the deserving poor'. Edith Sitwell's poem 'Still falls the rain', a meditation on the air raids in London in 1940, speaks of Jesus' compassion even with our self-inflicted pain, and with the pain of all his creation:

> He bears in His heart all wounds – those of the light that died,
> The last faint spark
> In the self-murdered heart, the wounds of the sad
> uncomprehending dark,
> The wounds of the baited bear –
> The blind and weeping bear whom the keepers beat
> On his helpless flesh ... the tears of the hunted hare.

How is this related to the experience of eucharistic adoration?

*　*　*

Let us return to the Norwegian Christian newspaper I mentioned at the end of the previous chapter. I have no idea what those responsible for the layout may have had in mind. But surely one could interpret the striking juxtaposition of the Pope's Mass and the many tragic public and private events of the contemporary world as *a sign of solidarity which gives us hope*. In the eucharist celebrated in the open air of a modern city, Christ is present at the very heart of the public world – not only in the special sacred spaces of cathedrals and monasteries, important as these are for the nourishing of our faith. And he is present offering his compassion to all those who suffer. He says that human existence, despite all the apparent hopelessness of the spirals of violence and destruction, is not meaningless: 'I am with you always, to the close of the age' (Mt 28:20). His solidarity with us gives us the right to hope.

'Hope that is seen is not hope,' says Paul (Rm 8:24). This is why Jesus always refuses to grant the disciples' requests for specific information about the future: 'Tell us, when will this be, and what will be the sign that all these things are about to be accomplished?' (Mk 13:4); 'When they had come together, they asked him, "Lord, is this the time when you will restore the kingdom to Israel?" He replied, "It is not for you to know the times or periods that the Father has set by his own authority"' (Acts 1:6f.). He does not tell us how or when things will be made right, or even whether they will be made right at all, here on earth. It is enough for us that we have his compassionate presence with us, as our fellow pilgrim on the road to Emmaus, our fellow sufferer in Auschwitz and the cancer hospice, to give us hope.

My own experience of eucharistic adoration has often taken the form of a deep assurance of the Lord's compassion, sometimes with those for whom I pray, sometimes with myself in my own suffering or uncertainty. To expose oneself to the rays of his love, and to let these rays play over all those who labour and are heavy-laden, is to receive his assurance that he is with us in our suffering, and that he will heal us. When and how he heals us, is his affair: 'it is not for you to know the times or periods ...'.

This hope empowers our intercession.

8

INTERCESSION

The prayer of petition has often been criticised by Christians who see it as an inferior, self-centred form of prayer: they urge that I should be content with adoring God for his own sake and thanking him. The only acceptable context in which I may make myself a theme of my prayer is the confession of my sins. I should not be trying to 'get something out of' my relationship to him.

The answer to all such objections is very brief: the word of God *commands* us over and over again to bring our petitions to God, and this is itself an act of adoration, since it is the acknowledgement of his love and his power. Thus intercession finds a natural place in prayer before the Blessed Sacrament.

We must always guard against over-spiritualising the spiritual life! Nothing that concerns my existence is 'unworthy' of inclusion in my prayer. If I need a job, if I need money, if I want someone to share my life with, then of course I should pray for these things. If my dog is sick, then of course I should pray for the dog – for what kind of a God would be indifferent to the suffering of his creatures? I have occasionally met the objection here that Jesus came only to redeem human beings, and that therefore prayer for animals is out of place. We need not discuss here the theological question of the eternal destiny of animals, which was rejected by St Thomas (d.1274) on somewhat one-sidedly rational grounds – he might perhaps have argued differently if he had had a dog himself. It suffices in our context to note that St Isaac of Nineveh (d.c. 700), most exalted of all the mystics in Christian history, wrote that the compassionate Christian heart should lead one to pray even for the wild animals and reptiles!

Apart from such arguments, there are specifically modern factors that make the prayer of petition and intercession difficult today, and I should like to discuss these at somewhat greater length.

Without faith in the power and the love of God, there can be no intercession. This is why the cultural climate of modern secularised societies, in which belief in God's active working is progressively eliminated from one sphere of life after another, is inevitably a climate that makes the prayer of petition difficult. If we no longer expect God to act in his world, it makes no sense to ask him to do so!

There is a kind of creeping atheism which we breathe in all the time, without noticing how it affects our perceptions both of public political events and of the private events of our own lives. The Old Testament takes for granted the principle that God's will and interventions can be discerned in Israel's history, even if there may be acute disagreement about the correct interpretation of specific events (for an example of such a dispute, see the conflict between the prophets Jeremiah and Hananiah in Jeremiah 28: *both* say, 'Thus says the Lord of hosts, the God of Israel ...'). But virtually all Catholics today would find it very odd if it were claimed that one could so clearly discern God's will and interventions in modern democratic politics that (for example) the result of a presidential or a parliamentary election could be taken as 'God's will for the people'. We do still pray for God's guidance of our leaders, and we pray for peace in the world. But we believe less and less genuinely in a God who is actively involved in what goes on, and who steers events. God has been eliminated from our public discourse, so that the 'religious' dimension of politics is limited in practice to what the participants agree in defining as ethical questions – recent examples are whether the Gulf War of 1991 could be called a 'just war', the protection or exploitation of the natural environment, and society's evaluation of the individual's rights (for example, on the issues of abortion or euthanasia). But in these debates – unlike the debate between Jeremiah and Hananiah 'in the presence of the priests and all the people who were standing in the house of the Lord' – the time is long past when one could presuppose a universal agreement on the existence of a God whose word communicates his will for our conduct. Such a God may still be mentioned in national constitutions, but in reality he has been totally evacuated from the public world.

The same creeping atheism has its effects on the private dimension of life too, so that most of us have to a great extent eliminated God's active and loving providence from our daily existence. This may be in part because we are rather afraid of him – 'The one who is near me is near the fire' – and want to keep him at a safe distance from us. But mostly it is because we lack faith that he really has the power to act and that we could genuinely experience his working.

This is, of course, nothing so tremendously new for Christians. We may recall here (in the West) the Anglican Bishop Butler's rebuke of John Wesley two hundred years ago: 'Sir, the pretending to extraordinary revelations and gifts of the Holy Ghost is a horrid thing, a very horrid thing', or (in the East) the polemical vigour with which St Simeon the New Theologian (d.1022) and St Seraphim of Sarov (d.1833) had to insist to their contemporaries that the aim of Christian existence was precisely to *experience* the Holy Spirit. The modern variant is based on what used to be called (before quantum physics altered the picture) the 'scientific worldview', which was understood to make God superfluous as a hypothesis to explain events in the autonomously functioning world. Some version of this worldview has left deep marks on the whole of our culture, so that many Christians today have great difficulties with the miraculous, whether in the biblical narratives about a Jesus who walked on the water, or in the Church's requirement of demonstrable miracles in the canonisation process, or in accounts of healings in charismatic groups. We have in fact done the same as the King of France in 1732 when he closed the cemetery of Saint-Médard, where the crowds had been streaming to the grave of the Jansenist deacon Francis de Pâris: *we have forbidden God to work miracles.* Indeed, we have forbidden him to work at all in our world!

Thus the challenge to faith is inevitably also a challenge to intercessory prayer, which we might formulate as follows: am I not importing God into the world, if I ask for his help?

Faith's answer to this, in brief terms, is that God is no absentee landlord, no creator who just sets things in motion and then retires from active involvement. He is always in the world, acting through the structures which he himself created. The difference between a 'miracle' and a 'normal event' lies in our perception of the divine action, not in his.

* * *

'We do not know how to pray as we ought,' says Paul (Rm 8:26). This is not least because the prayer of petition always involves two mysteries, namely divine freedom and human freedom. Put very simply, this means that I can never know with absolute certainty what the will of God is in any particular situation; I may pray for something in the sincere conviction that it is the best outcome, but he may well see that something else would be better. But even when I can be sure that my prayer is certainly in accord with his will, for example when I pray for peace and reconciliation, the answering of my prayer depends on the freedom of the combatants – a freedom which God always respects. My prayer opens a door through which God can act, but in this case he has chosen to let his own freedom be bound by that of his creatures. In a very profound sense, then, 'we do not know how to pray as we ought'.

The Bible teaches us by precept and by example that we should bring our petitions to God. Indeed, Jesus uses very drastic language to emphasise how vital it is 'to pray always and not to lose heart', when he compares the Father to an unjust judge who is finally worn down by the pleas of a widow and agrees to give her justice 'so that she may not wear me out by continually coming'. The lesson is clear: 'Listen to what the unjust judge says. And will not God grant justice to his chosen ones who cry to him day and night? Will he delay long in helping them? I tell you, he will quickly grant justice to them' (Lk 18:1ff.).

There are no universally valid rules about how we should make intercession. Sometimes the Holy Spirit will tell us whom we should pray for, and we ought always to follow such promptings. Time and again we find confirmation later on that a person for whom we prayed needed special strength and grace precisely at that hour, or that someone was moved to pray for us precisely at the hour when we needed God's help. Sometimes our prayer will be for the whole world without any distinctions, as we read in one of the fourth-century Macarian homilies: 'Sometimes they are, as it were, in grief and lamentation for the human race, and pouring out prayers for the whole race of Adam, they give way to tears and grief, burning with the love of the Spirit for mankind. At another time they are inflamed by the Spirit with such joy that, were it possible, they would take all mankind, good and bad, into their hearts.'

But perhaps our prayer can simply take the form of the last words of Blessed Niels Stensen as he lay dying: *Jesus, sis mihi Jesus,* 'Jesus, be Jesus to me', be for me 'Yahweh saves'. We can include wordlessly in the rich simplicity of this invocation all those we wish to hold up to the love of the Saviour who can make the broken whole. He knows what each one needs, and he loves each one with the total gift of his self. Our act of intercession not only calls on his love: it is itself the instrument his love employs to help his brothers and sisters.

* * *

Most of the fruit of our intercession is invisible. Only when the great harvest is gathered in at the end of the world, will we see what our prayer has been allowed to bring about, and it is good that it is so. In prayer, as in the rest of our life, 'we walk by faith, not by sight' (2 Co 5:7).

But sometimes I myself am the answer to my own prayer. It may be, for example, that I pray for 'all the lonely' and God answers this prayer by drawing to my attention one particular lonely person whom I could visit, or that I pray for 'the unity of all Christians' and God shows me some concrete step I myself could take to live in greater unity with other disciples of Jesus (whether inside or outside the fellowship of the Catholic Church). In this way, the encounter with the Lord allows him to send us out. We become the vessel that bears his sacred fire out from the sanctuary and into his world, where it can communicate a life-giving warmth that lets seeds buried in the winter earth burst forth into life. And so our lives, configured by silent eucharistic adoration to the compassion of Christ, bear fruit that is the best possible refutation of all the objections that can be brought against this kind of prayer.

SEEING THE LORD

Eucharistic adoration is the simple act of *looking at Jesus* exposed
in the sacrament of the altar. I should like to sum up this book
by reflecting on what the Gospels tell us about those who looked
at Jesus, and on the significant patterns this provides for our own
prayer.

'Look, the world has gone after him!' say the Pharisees (Jn
12:19). But what did seeing Jesus mean for these people who
'gathered by the thousands, so that they trampled on one another'
(Lk 12:1)? In one important sense, we could say that very many
of those who saw Jesus did not really see *him*. They saw what
Jesus could do for them through his teaching or his healing
activity, or what he could supply them with through a miracle –
'Sir, give us this bread always!' is the cry of the crowd who have
eaten of the loaves and fishes (Jn 6:34). Luke has a striking
example of this attitude in the story of the ten lepers healed on
the border between Samaria and Galilee (17:11ff.). Only one
returns to thank Jesus, who then exclaims: 'Were not ten made
clean? But the other nine, where are they?' The nine personify an
attitude towards Jesus that wants something from him, but
completely overlooks him as a man with whom one might enter
a personal relationship of love.

Another motive would be even less likely to lead to a positive
encounter, namely simple curiosity. I remember once, while I was
waiting at Rome's Fiumicino airport, noticing a tremendous
surge of people in the arrivals area. 'She's coming! She's coming!'
they cried to each other. I was caught up in the enthusiasm,
although I had no idea who 'she' might be. The tension grew, and
we all pressed forward to get a good view – myself included,
although I still did not understand why I was part of this
particular crowd, who were too excited to tell me anything, but
just kept shouting: 'She's coming!' Finally she emerged, and they
cried: 'She's here!' It was Sophia Loren. Everyone began to cheer

and applaud. The celebrity smiled graciously and departed. No one had tried to speak to her or to grab her hand. It was obviously quite enough for them *to have seen her.*

Those who came to see Sophia Loren at the airport did not come looking for a religious message. They did not come looking for healing. They simply came to see a celebrity, and no doubt they enjoyed telling their families and their friends afterwards about the experience (just as I myself enjoyed telling the story at supper in the monastery I was visiting).

Many of the people the Gospels tell us about must have had exactly the same motivation when they thronged around Jesus. This is certainly true of King Herod, who 'had been wanting to see him for a long time, because he had heard about him and was hoping to see him perform some sign' (Lk 23:8). Herod did not get his wish, but many others who were merely curious about the famous carpenter from Nazareth doubtless did get theirs. But nothing more. Seeing Jesus made no essential difference to their lives.

* * *

Doubtless our experience of seeing the Lord in eucharistic adoration *could* be that of Herod and the crowds, if we were to approach this form of prayer in the same superficial spirit. Ideally, however, our experience ought to be that of the tax-collector Zacchaeus in Jericho (Lk 19:1ff.). Initially, it is true, there is no spiritual profundity in what he does: 'He was trying to see who Jesus was', writes Luke, with no indication of any deeper wish in Zacchaeus' heart than in the hearts of the rest of the crowd, who block his view and force him to climb a sycamore tree 'to see him, because he was going to pass that way.' But when Zacchaeus gets his wish and sees Jesus, it does not leave his life unchanged. For what he sees is not a mere celebrity whom he can admire from a safe distance, but *someone who sees him* and knows his heart, someone who invites him to enter a personal relationship. And when he accepts this invitation, nothing can be the same as before:

'When Jesus came to the place, *he looked up* and said to him,

"Zacchaeus, hurry and come down; for I must stay at your house today." So he hurried down and was happy to welcome him ... Zacchaeus stood there and said to the Lord, "Look, half of my possessions, Lord, I will give to the poor, and if I have defrauded anyone of anything, I will pay back four times as much." Then Jesus said to him, "Today salvation has come to this house, because he too is a son of Abraham. For the Son of Man came to seek and to save the lost."'

Two points are especially important here. First, Zacchaeus in his tree is exposed to the Lord – Jesus does not need to be told who he is, or what sort of a man he is. But he does not reproach the tax collector, although he is a notorious 'sinner'. He simply asks Zacchaeus to invite him into his house. Today, when we see the Lord exposed in the sacrament of the altar, we too see someone who sees us and knows our heart. Even if we have not defrauded the poor as spectacularly as Zacchaeus had done ('he was a chief tax collector *and was rich*', says Luke), nevertheless we have no lack of sins of our own. But he does not condemn us: he invites us to enter a personal relationship by opening the door of our heart so that he may be our guest today.

Second, the experience of the compassion of Jesus, who forgives him and readmits him to the family of Abraham (from which his activity as tax collector had excluded him), leads Zacchaeus by an inherent logic to display this same compassion to others. He does not limit himself to the requirements of justice, by restoring what he has stolen. He goes even further: 'Half of my possessions, Lord, I will give to the poor!' So with us. Our experience of the boundless compassion of the Lord leads us by an inherent logic to *live* this same compassion with all who suffer, to be creative in finding ways to show them our love and our help.

And so Jesus will be able to say to each one of us: 'Today salvation has come to this house.' For each of us will have accepted the Lord's call to become his beloved disciple. And in the power of this love, we will be sent out as people whose lives bear witness to the truth of the divine promise: 'See, I am making all things new' (Rv 21:5).

* * *

Another narrative sheds light on what 'seeing Jesus' meant then: 'Now among those who went up to worship at the festival were some Greeks. They came to Philip, who was from Bethsaida in Galilee' (and therefore spoke Greek), 'and said to him, "Sir, we wish to see Jesus." Philip went and told Andrew; then Andrew and Philip went and told Jesus' (Jn 12:20ff.).

John describes here a procedure with which we are very familiar. The more important someone is, the more difficult it is to have the opportunity for a personal encounter. We know that we must go through the appropriate channels if we want to speak in private with a bishop or a leading politician. It is even more complicated, and in practice usually completely impossible, to get private access to the Pope or the President of the United States or the superstars of the entertainment world. There are many people employed precisely to protect the privacy of the great, and this is why there was such an outcry a few years ago when a man broke into Buckingham Palace and made his way to the Queen's bedroom for a conversation with her: how could such an immediate access be possible, when security officers were supposed to prevent it?

John shows us the apostles functioning as secretaries or bodyguards who screen applicants for a private audience with Jesus. Philip is apparently not sufficiently high in rank to make the decision on his own, so he has to consult Andrew (who always takes precedence over Philip when the names of the Twelve are listed). We see the same situation, when 'people were bringing little children to him in order that he might touch them; and the disciples spoke sternly to them' (Mk 10:13). Here, the disciples are overruled by Jesus himself. But the point remains valid: those who 'wished to see Jesus' had no direct access to him. They had to go through the appropriate channels.

Is this one of the reliable images and significant patterns the Bible gives us to guide us in our own relationship with Jesus? Does this show us what happens in eucharistic adoration today?

Fortunately, the answer to this question is no. John's scene depicts the situation before the Resurrection, when Jesus was necessarily localised in only one place at a time. He accepted for himself all the limitations inherent in a normal human existence, which meant being born and taking all the time needed to grow up and 'increase in wisdom' (Lk 2:52). He did not work miracles to satisfy his own hunger by turning stones into loaves of bread. He did not ask his Father for twelve legions of angels to fight off those who were arresting him in Gethsemane. He did not work a miracle to unfasten his hands and feet from the Cross, even when the chief priests challenged him to do so. His signs and wonders were only for others, not for himself. And so it was not possible for him, as a genuine human being under the conditions of the incarnation, to be simultaneously present in many places. This meant that access to him was necessarily limited to those who could see him with their own eyes. Others could hear about him, but they had no chance of meeting him or loving him in a personal way.

Let me emphasise once again that word 'personal'. It is certainly possible to feel a genuine love for someone whom one has never met. When King Olav V of Norway died in January 1991, the park in front of the royal palace in Oslo was unexpectedly transformed into a kind of chapel of remembrance by the thousands of Norwegians who brought red roses and lit candles which they stuck in the snow. Many children and adults left poems and greeting cards alongside their roses and candles, thanking the dead king for what he had meant to them. In the days leading up to his funeral, every shop window in the city centre had a portrait of King Olav draped in black crêpe. None of this was ordered by the state authorities (unlike the public weeping of the North Koreans seen on television after the dictator Kim Il Sung died in 1994). Nor was it the expression of an intellectual adherence to the system of constitutional monarchy; scarcely any Norwegians could be described as monarchists. What happened in January 1991 was the spontaneous expression of very deep feelings that were evoked by the passing of a king who had shown outstanding devotion to the service of his people in war and peace.

This love was perfectly genuine; King Olav is said to have told a visiting American statesman who had commented on the absence of security in Oslo that he had 'four million bodyguards' to protect him anyway, so why should he need the men with dark glasses and guns? But for virtually all who mourned, this could never have become a personal love between friends, since they never had the opportunity to meet the king in private. In the geographically localised reality of human life, mutual personal love requires that we meet one another and communicate with one another.

This kind of encounter with Jesus was of necessity limited to a very small number of people. This is why the first disciples, those who had known Jesus before his Passion and who formed the nucleus of his Church after the Resurrection, were so few, 'about one hundred and twenty' according to Acts 1:15, or 'more than five hundred', if we prefer Paul's more optimistic estimate (1 Co 15:6). But this limitation is completely abolished by the Resurrection. Jesus can no longer be seen by the eyes of the body. But the eyes of faith can see him everywhere. We do not need to go through an apparatus of secretaries and bodyguards to snatch five minutes with him. St Ignatius of Antioch (d.107) puts the liberating paradox in this way in his Letter to the Romans: 'Our God Jesus Christ is all the more visible now that he is in the Father.' He can be seen in the host, and eucharistic adoration gives us the opportunity for a private encounter that can last as long as we wish.

* * *

At the same time, this is a very particular kind of 'seeing'. God tells Moses, 'You cannot see my face; for no one shall see me and live' (Ex 33:20), and this remains true in the New Covenant: 'no one has ever seen or can see' the God who 'dwells in unapproachable light' (1 Tm 6:16). This means that although Jesus does indeed make it possible for us to see the Father – 'Whoever has seen me has seen the Father' (Jn 14:9) – he does not remove the dimension of *longing* from the life of faith, as if seeing him were the full satisfaction of faith's desires. On the contrary: we are allowed to see Jesus here on earth, in a genuine act of seeing, precisely in order that we shall *desire* even more strongly to see him face-to-face in heaven.

The same point is made in the Book of Sirach (24:19ff.), employing the image of hunger and eating: 'Come to me, you who desire me, and eat your fill of my fruits', says the divine Wisdom, 'for the memory of me is sweeter than honey, and the possession of me sweeter than the honeycomb.' This certainly sounds like the full satisfaction of the human desire for God, but in fact it is precisely the opposite that is true! For this is not a meal that satisfies our hunger, but paradoxically, one that makes the guests even more ravenous: 'Those who eat of me *will hunger for more,* and those who drink of me *will thirst for more.'* 'Open your mouth wide and I will fill it,' says God (Ps 81:10). But he fills it in such a way that we still have to ask him each day for 'our daily bread'.

Jesus tells us several times in the Gospels that those who ask will receive. But only those who are aware of their need will ask. The worst thing that can happen to us in the spiritual life is that our longing dies, for if we imagine that our hands are already full, we are not going to stretch them out to the Lord – and he will not be able to fill them with his gifts. Those without longing live completely divorced from reality, like the church in Laodicea: 'You say, "I am rich, I have prospered, and I need nothing." You do not realise that you are wretched, pitiable, poor, blind and naked' (Rv 3:17).

Every encounter with Jesus here on earth is meant to kindle our desire for the eternal encounter with him in heaven. This principle applies to eucharistic adoration, and that is why St Thomas concludes his great hymn for the feast of Corpus Christi with two strophes which were an invariable element of the service of benediction when I was growing up: *O salutaris hostia,* translated as follows by James Quinn:

O Priest and Victim, Lord of Life,
Throw wide the gates of Paradise!
We face our foes in mortal strife;
Thou art our strength! O heed our cries!

To Father, Son and Spirit blest,
One only God, be ceaseless praise!
May he in goodness grant us rest
In heaven, our home, for endless days!

I have written above that eucharistic adoration is not an escapist form of prayer, but a meeting with Jesus that sends us out into his world as bearers of his compassion. The deepest reason for this is that the adoration of Jesus in the host makes us profoundly conscious that – whatever else we may happen to have in the way of health or money or possessions or power, and so on – we are fundamentally indigent. We lack the most important thing of all, which is of course no 'thing', but the Lord himself, for whom we long. And the knowledge of this unsatisfied longing makes us aware of our solidarity with all those who suffer from unsatisfied longings – whether these are material or emotional or spiritual. Thus, when we come to them and seek to help, we are not playing Lady Bountiful. We stand with them, on their level.

The final words of the Mass, *Ite, missa est,* are rendered in a curiously tame fashion in all the translations I know. For example, we have three alternatives in the English missal: 'Go in the peace of Christ', or 'The Mass is ended, go in peace', or 'Go in peace to love and serve the Lord'. No doubt it is good to end the liturgy with such sentiments, but the real meaning of the ancient words is surely something much more vigorous: 'Get out of here! You are dismissed!' This is because there is an inner dynamic in the celebration of the eucharist that kindles in us a peremptory longing, a desire for Christ, that propels us out of the church building and into the world.

The same is true of the silent prayer of eucharistic adoration. Nothing commits us more deeply and ineradicably to help those who suffer – in all the endless varieties of human pain – than this prayer in which we expose ourselves to the fire of Christ's love and immerse ourselves in the abyss of his compassion. I hope that those who have accompanied me in the reflections in this book will open themselves to this experience of the fire and the abyss, and let themselves be sent out by the Master who is here and is calling for us.